Marry Me Stop

Marry Me Stop

REGINA LANDOR

ISBN: 1508841047
ISBN 13: 9781508841043
Library of Congress Control Number: 2015909488
CreateSpace Independent Publishing Platform
North Charleston, South Carolina

"I've learned that people will forget what you've said and what you did. But people will never forget how you made them feel."
Maya Angelou

Acknowledgments:

I would like to thank all who took an interest in this story, but more importantly, those who took an interest in my mother. I feel so much gratitude to everyone who helped care for her, in the past and in recent years. So many people reached out to her in a loving way, even if all that meant was sitting next to her at a party and asking her a question. I felt supported by those gestures, and they meant the world to her.

Judy Wolf Anderson, thank you for your valuable input. Thank you, Heather Antti, for offering me your editorial expertise. To all of my siblings, I thank you for your support and enthusiasm about this book. Of course, you are all an intrinsic part of this story.

Victor Sperber unreservedly helped fill in the details of his and my mom's home-life. Thanks, Uncle Vic! I wholeheartedly thank Elaine Bickford, whose friendship with my mother has lasted over half a century, and whose unwavering loyalty facilitated me in writing this book. I thank my two boys from the bottom of my heart for being there on this journey we took with Grandma Mimi. Thank you Billy Woodward, my husband. I have so much gratitude for the sacrifices you've made and the care you've given. We all do. Above all, I thank my mother, Miriam Anna Sperber Landor, who has been a model of generosity, courage, and love her whole, long life.

For Billy, with love and gratitude

Prologue

This morning I was standing in my kitchen about to make cookies. From the open wall in the kitchen that leads to the dining room, I was watching my mom. She was pacing. Her shoulders were hunched. Her face wore an angry expression. She stopped her pacing and put her hands on the counter between us.

I was scrolling through my computer, looking for that recipe. I paused and looked up at my mom who was now watching me. She was staring at me but she wasn't looking at me. She was deep in thought, in the place in her mind where she goes to worry. The weight of the world—the weight of her entire life—was visible in her face right now.

I looked down at my computer and stopped searching for the recipe. I switched to iTunes and scrolled down to find her music. I clicked on her song and looked up to watch her face. I watched her and waited for it. One beat. Two beats. Then it came. Clean and loud and important, Anne Murray's voice slid out of the computer. On the first, long drawn-out word, "*Lord,*" my mother raised her head and without pause, a smile covered her face completely. She looked at me and started mouthing the words. *Lord, I hope this day is good.* This time, she could see me. Even though I smiled back at her, my eyes welled up with tears. My mom stood still and became one with the music. There was nothing between her and that song. The music carried her worries out the door. All she heard and felt was the music. She sang and she swayed and she smiled.

She came into the kitchen and pulled up a chair. *I'm feeling empty like you knew I would,* she sang. I turned on the oven. I got out the mixing bowl. I beat the sugar and the butter. I measured the dry ingredients. *I should be thankful, Lord, I know I should.* My mom's voice lifted. I sang along, too, as I pulled out the oats and the raisins. And I was taking the words to heart. I was thinking about how I yelled at my kids this morning because they were going to miss the bus if they didn't hurry, and they wouldn't hurry. I was thinking about how I want a second chance. I want a shot at being more kind. At being a better mom. At being a better daughter. I hope the rest of this day is good, but I hope tomorrow is better. My mom, at this stage in her life, deserves to be honored. I don't want to get mad at her. *Lord, I hope this day is good.* The music filled the small space of our kitchen.

"Regina, you're the best mother in the world. I don't know anyone who takes care of their kids like you do."

"Oh mom. Stop. Here, have a cookie." I gave her a hug, too. This is part of my second chance. Taking care of her, making her cookies, honoring her. Writing a book about her life will also honor her.

Marry Me Stop

We live in Dhaka, Bangladesh. We are in the Foreign Service and this is the first time that my mother has lived with us. A friend sparked the idea. Raenette came to visit us in Chicago. She brought her 80-something mother-in-law, Charlene, who has been my mother's friend for years. They had not seen each other in a very long time, but it seemed that Charlene recognized and responded to her old friend, Miriam, even though her Alzheimer's seemed pretty advanced. My mother was staying with us for the weekend, away from her retirement home, which she loathed.

They sat on our couch and Raenette took care of Charlene, answering questions where she faltered, laughing along with her, being a companion. As I listened to Raenette describe her life with her husband and Charlene, I was amazed at the sacrifices that she was making to do this. But Raenette didn't present it that way. She presented it more like it was her responsibility and something she gracefully accepted.

That visit planted the seed for me. My husband, Billy, was serving one year in Afghanistan. Our two boys and I were waiting and eager for him to come home so that we could all be together and prepare for our next assignment, Bangladesh. We spoke on the phone or Skyped every day. During one of those conversations, I asked him what it would be like to take my mother with us. He did not think about it for very long before saying, "Yeah. If it were my mother it's what I would want to do."

I remember a conversation I had with my sister, Talitha. She knew all about living with my mom, who is her stepmother.

Before the cycle of retirement homes set in, Talitha lovingly took care of her for a year, setting up house for her on her farm in North Carolina. But it was a hard year for my mom. She felt isolated, despite how much Talitha and her partner included her in their lives. My mom didn't want to be on a farm. She wanted shops and bookstores and libraries outside her front door. I started to cry on the phone with Talitha, telling her I don't know how I'm going to leave my mom in her retirement home. Our next posting in Dhaka was for four years.

A thought that kept recurring was that if we want to be kind to people, we should be kind to those people who are right in front of us. My mom was the one person closest to me who needed more kindness extended to her than anyone else I knew. I kept thinking about Raenette. If she can take care of her mother-in-law, I can take care of my mother.

My mother is funny, warm, remarkably kind and generous, and sometimes a pain in the ass. She's stubborn; she won't listen to reason because she's got dementia and she can't; she repeats herself relentlessly; she has a paper trail that begins on her dresser in her bedroom and if Billy and I didn't clear it out every now and then, it would take over the house; she writes incessant notes about the same things—usually her banking; she uses our phone to call people in the middle of the day in Dhaka—the middle of the night in America; and she questions me again and again about her medication and how it's causing a "reaction," as if I'm the guilty one prescribing it.

But somehow deciding that she live with us seemed like an easy decision. As hard as it has been at times, it's mostly been easy, even though we have definitely made sacrifices. My mother needs to be taken care of—help with hearing aids, help with getting shoes on, told to eat, told to shower—so that I often feel like I am taking care of a child, that I have three children and not just two. We've altered plans and trips; we've struggled emotionally with her delusions; have feared for our safety when she's at her most delusional; have had the responsibility of ensuring she gets the right medication; have had to find doctors and caretakers so she's not alone when I leave the house; have been swept up in long, twisted explanations about where her belongings are, where all her money is, and always it comes back to the jewelry: where's my such-and-such a necklace? (It's somewhere in her room where she's hidden it.)

Despite all of that—and I mean this sincerely and whole-heartedly—it's mostly been gratifying and rewarding sharing this time in her life with her. I'm writing this book, in part, to point out ways in which having my mother live with us and join our family has been gratifying.

When I asked my mother if she wanted to come live with us in one of the poorest countries on the planet, without a moment's hesitation she said, "When should I start packing?" My mother has always been game for adventure, and at 78 years old, she was still ready to roll the dice. We thought we'd need to plop her in a wheel-chair during our nearly 24-hour trip to Dhaka—but no. She kept up with us in the airports and the rush to catch the planes every step of the way, didn't complain once, and like any traveler who has a spirit of moving forward in her bones, she eased into her new liv-ing situation on the other side of the world like it was no big deal.

All she cared about was that she was with family.

Then

Chapter One

The image in my mind is all grainy, like a sepia photo from the 1940s. I know there was a yard and children playing, and there was probably a thud when the refrigerator came down. It wouldn't have been large, like the tall rectangular refrigerators we have in our kitchens now. More short and squat. And they probably called it an icebox. But it was big enough to break a leg. Her older brothers may have heard the bone in her leg snap, and one of them may have run back to the house to tell their mom. This is how I imagine it.

She was taken to the hospital on a bus with her mother comforting her, her mother who knew how to take care of a child. She had given birth to twelve of them. One of them, around the time of the refrigerator, was stillborn and the other children cried when their mother came home from the hospital without her, and they called her a blue baby. Another baby was born but lived for only one day.

On this trip to the hospital, my mother was very young. She was afraid of being left alone at the hospital, but she would have to be. Her mother could not spend the night with Miriam. My mother whimpered, perhaps in discomfort, most definitely in fear. This may have been the first time she had ever been alone in her life. After her mother left her and she was alone crying in her bed, the nurse on duty said to her sharply, "Shut up." Little Miriam slid under the bed sheets and tried to stifle her tears.

Her mother greeted her on the hospital ward the next day with a box. She smiled down at her precious daughter and saw the unexpected look in her eyes. Living under the duress of poverty, and an uncompromisingly stern father at home, gifts of any kind were practically an unknown.

Miriam paused before opening the box, still not ready to fully believe the gift was for her. Her mother nudged her to open it, smiling down at her little girl. Miriam lifted the lid and as she did, her tiny mouth opened and she let out a faint gasp. A brand new pair of shoes! They were not her brothers' old pairs. They were not handouts from a neighbor. They were not her father's old shoes, big and floppy, which she once had to wear to school, dragging her feet in shame. They were not ugly. These shoes on her lap in front of her were tan and glossy and beautiful. And they were hers. Her first pair—leather and with dark, new laces, not frayed but with a plastic tip on the end of each lace.

Miriam beamed up at her mother, still not believing these were really for her. But she put one on anyway and looked down at her legs. It looked a little silly, with one shoe on her foot and the other foot wrapped in plaster. She smiled up at her mother, stood up and hugged her, and together they walked out of the hospital, Miriam walking slowly with her leg feeling strange and heavy, carrying in her hand the bag that contained the box that contained her other new shoe. Her heart beat with excitement at the thought of showing her new shoes to her big sister. She knew that her sister would be happy for her and on the way out of the hospital, she thought about what little thing she could give her so that she would also have a gift.

They took the long bus ride home, mother and daughter. Maybe it was the newness of it all, of riding a bus together, or the preoccupation of what lay ahead— remembering where to disembark, facing father and husband, greeting the children—that made them forget.

At some point too late, they remembered. Maybe it was when they were off the bus and watching it disappear around a corner, and Miriam too lame to run after it. Maybe they realized it together, both putting their hands up to their mouths and gasping at what they'd done. Maybe it was when they arrived home and Miriam wanted to show off her new gift and she went to find her mother to ask for the box.

However it unfolded, the sinking feeling that arrived in the bottom of Miriam's stomach when she realized what had happened stayed with her long after her cast was removed. Her other shoe had been left on the bus. Her mother went to a neighbor's to borrow a telephone and called the bus company, but it was too late. Her brand new shoe never found its match. It was gone forever.

Chapter Two

My mother was born in Newark, New Jersey in 1934. She already had four older siblings, Victor, David, Ruth, and Joseph. Victor, the oldest of ten children, was instrumental in piecing together for me some of the harsh realities of their life. He was born in 1929 and the Depression was soon to catch up to their parents. Around the time Miriam was born, their father, now with five children, lost everything. Victor remembers men coming to their home with rifles demanding that they leave. Their father was a minister with an ample following at the time. When the authorities demanded that he leave his home, he gave his car to a parishioner on condition that he get them somewhere safe. My mother remembers being told that all of the belongings they could take with them were thrown into a wheelbarrow.

They arrived at a home called Father Divine's Place of Worship, in Philadelphia. Father Divine was a black minister who fed them, clothed them, and kept them safe until they found another place to live. The family eventually made it back to Newark where they lived in a series of small apartments, paid for by Welfare. Their father refused to work. He held the government responsible for his losing everything, and now it was the government's turn to pay it all back.

Emil Otto Sperber was a fierce man with a set of convictions that he took with him to America on a ship from Lithuania in 1906. That was the same year that my grandmother was born—his future wife. When he was 18 years old, he left Lithuania—somehow—to escape conscription. He called himself a pacifist and all the stories that I ever heard about my grandfather set me to wondering early on how someone's belief system could conflict so drastically with one's actual behavior.

He had an idea to start what he called a "Love and Peace Movement." This was in the 1930s. My mother jokes that he was ahead of his time, talking about love and peace before the same revolution in the 1960s. But my grandfather's love and peace was wrapped all around the Bible, not drugs and music and free love. As a young man he ended up in Berea, Ohio where, coincidentally, my family moved a half a century later and where I grew up. He went to Seminary College at Baldwin Wallace College, in Berea, and later moved back east where electricity was coming down the road, as they said, on some of those eastern farms—and so were missionaries. That's how he met my grandmother, Edith Malwitz, a farmer's daughter.

He had all sorts of ideas of promoting his religious convictions. "Today we would call it marketing," my mother's brother, Victor, says. He built an altar in his home and used his children as his sounding board for his sermons. Edith played the piano and they sang hymns. They called him "Apostle," never Daddy. As in "Good night, Apostle." Only, they never said "Hello, Apostle." They were not allowed to use the word hello because of the reference to a place that bad children will go to if they do not behave—Hell. They were taught to say "Love and peace" when they greeted someone, and "Peace and love" when they said goodbye. He wrote signs with Biblical verses that he put on the window shades, in the windows, and all over the walls of the house. The children learned from memory and recited Biblical verses every Sunday.

I wonder under what duress they were commanded to do this. My mother has said all her life that her father took his frustrations out on his family, and Victor confirms this. He says, "He lost all of his worldly possessions and now with a bunch of kids running around he was losing control. His frustration turned to anger and he took it out on us. When we boys disobeyed he would have us lay on the seat of a chair. There he would beat us with a leather strap." Out of my mother's own guilt, maybe out of a sense of betraying him, she defends him, telling me that his goal in life of becoming a minister was never fulfilled. After the Depression, he also lost his following.

The relief that overcame my mother and her brothers and sisters at the words "In conclusion" during one of Apostle's long sermons was profound. His love and peace was choking her and her siblings nearly to death. How they must have squirmed. The outside calling to them, the voices of kids in the street playing ball.

Outside! The freedom to run. The freedom to play. How the sun and the wind and the air, and even the night, contrasted to their dark interior where radios were evil and tossed out the window, shattering on the pavement below. Where games were forbidden. Where a strict adherence to authority was the only way. He made them fear him. In return, they shunned him and they ran away.

The boys stayed out late and they wouldn't come home. When the social welfare authorities learned of the Sperber home life, they took action. The police picked up David and Joseph first. They were put in foster care, and then eventually put in separate homes. Victor says, "I, too, was sent to several foster homes around age ten. The last was on a small chicken farm where for the first time I witnessed a husband and wife hug each other."

Victor and David ran away from the foster homes and made it back, but one did not—Joseph. Like his namesake in the Bible, Joseph unintentionally wandered far and wide from the fold before eventually making his way back home. He was placed in another home, adopted, and grew up with another family. My mother remembers my grandmother sending him packages— clothes, mittens, hats, food—which he never received. Whoever was in charge of his case must have wanted all ties severed. Joseph grew up with the conviction that he had been abandoned, so like the Biblical character. He eventually married, gained wealth, divorced, lost his wealth, became an alcoholic, and died.

I had met all of my aunts and uncles growing up, on the occasional summer trip east to New Jersey and the Jersey Shore. It wasn't until I was in my early 20s that I met Joseph. It was at a party at my Aunt Ann's house. I walked into the room and gave everyone a hug, the last person being Joseph. Then I did a double take. Joseph looked just like everyone else there, that strong family resemblance in every aspect of his face, the Sperber nose, the wide, open face. But I looked back at Joseph and said, "Wait—I've never met you before!" He, and everyone else in the room burst out laughing, revealing that good humor which so characterized my mother's brothers and sisters. Joseph had waited until his adoptive parents died before reuniting with his biological family, and it took all those years to do so. A few years before his death, he called my mom many times seeking comfort and she patiently listened to his woes. It dismayed her to hear those clinking ice cubes on the other end.

Edith Malwitz, my mother's mother, was of German descent, born and raised on a farm in Union, New Jersey. According to my mother, Edith's mother, my great grandmother, was a religious zealot and an unkind woman who was never nice to Edith's children and apparently despised her husband, my grandfather. The only story I know of my grandmother when she was a child was of the time she was walking down the road and saw a woman sitting in a rocking chair on her front porch. Edith did not know this woman but went up to her anyway and asked if she could sit on her lap.

If the Sperber kids did not receive kindness from their grandmother, at least they did from their mother's father, a man my mother remembers with fondness. He extended his kindness to the whole family by helping them purchase a home in Cranford.

Marry Me Stop

Some relief came to the family during this time. For one, their father went to work. He got a job as a barber, which is also how he had earned his way through Seminary College in Berea. David and Victor were now back at the house, but not for long.

Those kids roamed everywhere around their new neighborhood in Cranford. My mother remembers leaving the house in the morning and her mother shouting after her and her siblings from the front door, "Come home when the lights turn on!" She and her older brothers and sister played baseball in a field and did not come home until well after dark. My mom says they were never given any warnings about danger. Her parents simply trusted those kids would be safe, even if that meant their running up to the railroad tracks to watch the trains go by. It was exciting, especially when soldiers coming home from the war were on some of those trains tossing little bags of candy at them from the train windows.

Once upon a time, a friend of the family gave my mother a cape. There is a black and white photo of her in that cape, standing on the steps of a house surrounded by some of her siblings and her mother standing behind them all. My mother looks about eight years old. She is smiling, and even in that picture I can sense the pride she felt in owning her cape. It made her feel like a princess.

At that point in her little life, she never had anything more beautiful than that cape. I imagine others admiring it. I imagine her wearing it wherever she went. She may have worn it to bed, even, for fear it may be gone in the morning. She had good reasons to be afraid of her father, who never let her and her siblings have anything that may have been considered frivolous. Her new cape was a thing that brought her joy in the bleakness of her family's poverty. She may have had to even conceal that joy for fear it would be snatched away. In the everyday uncertainty of where her next meal would come, and of her father's anger, her cape was her one, sure security blanket.

Her older sister, Ruth, didn't have a cape. There was nothing she owned to disguise her sorry excuse for school clothes. Their mother was forced to take extreme measures in dressing her many children. Either in an act of desperation, or a sudden stroke of ingenuity, she put the oldest daughter in a dress made out of used potato sacks, with a rope for a belt. And as soon as Ruth was old enough to drop out of school, she did.

Emil Otto Sperber's children were his only congregation in Cranford. So it's not surprising that those kids stayed away from home as much as possible. Once, my mother walked so far, she got a bit lost. She walked down her street, past the simple, two-story, wooden framed houses with porches and small yards, away from the railroad tracks and into town. She decided she'd take a bus home, so she waited by a bus stop and got on the next one. She asked the conductor where Winans Avenue is and he told her where to get off. Only, she didn't know she had to buy a ticket. He let her ride the bus anyway. She did not easily forget simple gestures of kindness that were extended to her during those years.

Victor was preparing to move out for good. He needed to get away from his father, whom he says was a tyrant. When his father got angry he would yell, "Get out!" so Victor did, living with his friends on and off. The very last time his father hit him was when Vic dared to punch him back. He was a teenager at the time and restless to do something with his life. World War II was just over and Victor wanted to join the Army, especially with the advantages of the GI Bill. He'd heard if he served in the Army, he could get free college tuition, and he wanted in on it. But he was only 17 and his father refused to sign for him. He was a conscientious objector, and continued calling himself a pacifist. Victor went back to the former Welfare authorities in Newark. He asked the state to adopt him as a guardian; they agreed and he joined the Army. His plan of escape changed his life. He later went to business school, started his own business, and had many years of success.

My mom and I are taking a walk in our new neighborhood in Dhaka, Bangladesh. It's a world away from her old neighborhood in Cranford, New Jersey. We are being careful where we step, avoiding potholes and garbage and mud and giving a wide berth to the stray dog. "She accepted her lot in life," my mom says of her older sister, as we talk about her childhood. "But she didn't have to, Mom," I tell her. "You didn't accept your lot in life. You made choices, just like she did. At every turn, Mom, you chose to better yourself." We talk about how the world can be divided into those who accept their lot in life, and those who do not.

If my mom had accepted her lot in life, I don't think there's a chance in a million that she'd be walking with her daughter under a canopy of tropical trees in South Asia.

Chapter Three

⟋

My mom watched out for her younger siblings. She wanted to protect them, Philip, Tim, Jonathon, Jimmy, and Ann. Being the middle child, my mother was the designated peacemaker. I think her siblings have felt indebted to her all of their lives for the care she showed them when they were young, living with a Bible thumping "pacifist" in a warring house, and the pent up fear and trembling.

She did what she could to stay out of the line of fire and avoid their father's wrath. But it wasn't always possible. A colleague once admonished my mother for continually saying, "I'm sorry." Stop being sorry all the time! she said to her.

I'm sorry! I'm sorry! I'm sorry! I won't do it again! she remembers saying when she was a child, but she never knew what she was saying sorry for. She remembers the belt and everyone lining up to get their beating. She remembers cowering under the bed and him coming after her with a long-handled broom.

Marry Me Stop

Slowly walking down the street one day, my mother says she looked up from her daydreaming and saw a large building. Something compelled her to enter, and she found herself in a large room filled with books. It was called a public library. The only book that was permitted inside her house was the Bible, so Miriam had to be very sneaky with those books she started to check out.

She fell in love with reading and read whenever she had the chance, and whenever she knew she wouldn't be caught. She had an ambition to become a secretary when she graduated high school, like the young woman she read about in a book she found at the library. The young woman in the book wore elegant, long, white gloves and worked as a private secretary for a rich man with whom she eventually started a romance, and my mom wanted to be just like her. Books may have been the safest place in the world to escape to when she was a child.

She got her first job at sixteen as a telephone operator. As a little girl, I loved hearing my mom imitate her younger self. "Number please?" she'd say in a cheerful voice. I was riveted as she recalled sitting in front of a big board that lit up when someone was making a call. She recorded long distance calls on a little pad of paper next to her. When there were no incoming calls, she and her girlfriend, Joanne, who also worked as an operator and sat at the end of the row, fooled the boss by pretending they were connecting numbers, but in fact were staring straight ahead at the board chatting away with each other. I can well imagine what they were talking about—boys, of course!

One Christmas, my mother bought orange crinkly paper made to look like a real fire and she assembled a little Christmas hearth in the living room corner. She wanted cheer in the house, particularly to please her younger siblings. But any attempt at beauty or creativity was squelched. When her father saw the hearth, he tore it down. I imagine her upstairs in her bedroom, hearing the carefully hung hearth being torn from the wall, holding her breath, trying not to cry.

She also bought a board game for her brother, Jonathon. He played with it, and it must have given him great joy. My mother stares into the distance as she recalls the coal-burning furnace in the basement. Their father must have seen Jonathon with his game. He must have witnessed the pleasure his young son was receiving from it, probably the only game he'd ever owned. And somewhere in his mind he equated this pleasure—this board game—as coming from the devil. It was taken from him and thrown in that furnace.

Miriam was the only child in a brood of ten that stayed in high school. She was on the yearbook committee and she was terrific at typing. A teacher started calling her Mimmie, and that caught on faster than Mimmie's words per minute. All her friends now started calling her Mim. She had some good friends. She was flirty and kind and boys probably liked her, too. She made an effort to look nice, despite the hand-me-downs she received from neighbors or friends.

When she was invited to a girlfriend's sweet-sixteen party, with the earnings from her job as telephone operator, she was able to buy her friend a present. She bought her a necklace. But when she got home and tried on the necklace herself, she decided she could not part with it. It was too beautiful. She considered the ramifications of not going to that party. How would her friend even know the necklace was intended for her? She could make up an excuse as to why she wasn't at the party. She could say that she was sick. Or that she forgot. Whatever she decided to tell her friend, my mother could not resist going to school the next day wearing that necklace, a thing that made her feel beautiful and special and maybe she even believed it would disguise her poverty. Her friend noticed the necklace and put two and two together. The shame never left my mother.

The friend didn't hold my mother's transgression against her, however. Many years later this friend told my mother that if it weren't for her, she wouldn't have gone to college. My mother encouraged those around her at a very early age.

I wonder if my mother shared some of her teenage angst with her own mother. As a teenager, did she talk with her? She doesn't talk about having heart-to-hearts, even though my mother refers to her mother as a saint. "Mother was an angel. And she never yelled." Maybe that's true, but with seven wild boys and ten kids in all to feed, that's really hard to imagine. But it is possible. That is also how I remember my grandmother—a woman with a profound love for others. It was devastating to have to feed an entire family with one chicken. But she knew how to stretch out a meal, saving the fat to fry up potato pancakes. They loved those potato pancakes.

When I think of my grandmother, who died when I was about ten and whom I only saw occasionally in my young life, I think of her softness. She was round and plump. She had soft, supple cheeks and her hugs were fierce. She could crush you with those arms of hers she just loved you so much. Her kitchen smelled of bacon and eggs—homey, comfort food. She shook when she laughed.

I was a very naughty little girl once. I followed my cousin Debby through my grandmother's kitchen and upstairs to the bathroom, walking past my grandmother and pretending to be nonchalant, but what I was really feeling was fear—that I would be found out and my grandmother would catch me being sneaky. Debby wanted to show me her cigarettes and how to smoke. We walked past my mother's old bedroom that she shared with her sister when she was little. There were twin beds in it still, a plain room with faded paint on the walls. We went into the bathroom and Debby lit the cigarette, puffed on it, and blew the smoke out the window. She showed me how to do it, too.

I had the feeling that I was killing something that day. If my grandmother were to know what I was doing, a bit of the light she had for me would be extinguished forever. But I pretended to my cousin that I didn't care. My grandmother used to sing the song "Jesus Loves the Little Children." I loved that song, but today, I hoped my grandmother would not find out what I was doing because if she did, Jesus wouldn't love me the same way anymore and neither would she. That I couldn't bear.

She never found out and she loved me just the same, always. I've wondered how such a loving person could have spent her life with a man whose personality contrasted so sharply with her own, even though I believe there must have been a glimmer of kindness in my grandfather, and maybe he mellowed somewhat as his children grew. The barbershop where he worked was smack next to a delicious-smelling bakery. He once came home with a whole box of sugar cookies for the family. My mother and some of her brothers met him at the bus stop at the end of the day to walk home with him. Victor says that sometimes it was only Mim who walked the long distance to greet him. They must have loved him, even as they yearned for his affirmation. When my mother graduated from high school in the spring of 1952, he and my grandmother came to the ceremony—she was the only child who finished school, after all—and treated her to ice cream at Howard Johnson's. His stoicism didn't allow for him to show it much, but he must have been so proud of his Miriam.

Chapter Four

⌒

Who wouldn't want to hire an attractive, tall, smart blond as a secretary? Deciding to hire my mom who had excellent secretarial skills must have been a no-brainer. She finally realized her ambition when she finished high school and got a job as a secretary at Standard Oil, only without the elegant, long, white gloves of her childhood romance novel.

In the summer of 1953 Miriam was nineteen years old. Was it at a nightclub that she met a lieutenant in the Navy who was subsequently stationed in Germany and feverishly wrote her passionate letters declaring his love? Maybe. She loved parties and nightclubs and drinking and posing for pictures. Albums that she kept from those years are filled with square black and white photos of her and her friends—girls and boys—posing on the beach, at cocktail parties, at the pool. Dave's full name and address are scrawled in all caps on a cocktail napkin. He wrote her about 20 letters, postcards, and telegrams, which she saved in a sturdy cardboard box with a metal clasp. All of his letters—and one rough draft of a reply to him—are tied up with a faded, pink ribbon.

They are downright steamy. In the earliest dated letter to her in the stack he writes,

At sea.

3 August 1953

Dearest Mim,

I'm going to write a bit tonight then finish this tomorrow—because I'm not sure just what I want to say. —Oh, I know what I want to say, clearly enough, but, perhaps it's not what I should say. I'm afraid my heart would dictate my words, not my head. I keep trying to think sensibly—my heart, I'm afraid, is not too sensible. But, then, perhaps you wouldn't mind if I were not too sensible if we could bring back the magic I felt when I held you close and I could see right into your eyes. You make my spine tingle, my hair stand on end, every fiber tuned to full pitch. To me, you are the most desirable creature I've ever met . . .

Poor guy. It could not have been easy, being on that ship with hundreds of other sailors, pining away for her. He is an ardent lover and his letters sound like a 1950s comic strip. He uses words like "golly" and "swell" and calls her "Hon" a lot. He begs her to show up during a stopover in New York, in one letter after another, and I find myself feeling relieved for his sake that it appears she finally does. But the seas are rough and missing her is no good.

Mim, this long-distance becoming acquainted is strictly for the birds! I know that I must see you again soon. You always say (write) just the right things, things I want so much to hear you say, things I want to hear you whisper to me! Is that bad? If so, then I'm a bad, bad boy! . . . Incidentally all the officers got a big kick out of your picture. They agree emphatically with me that nature has generously endowed you with the endearing young charms we love so much!

When he's not thinking about her body, maturity peeks through in his lusty letters. In between the rambling passion of how much he misses her, how he hopes to see her whenever his ship sails in, how beautiful and wonderful and sexy she is, he discusses Hemingway. My mother wonders if he's read "The Old Man and the Sea." He says the book, . . . *really rings a bell for me. It particularly held me since my home is in the "semi-tropics" and I love to fish and hunt. I've been through the Caribbean several times and the descriptions are perfect. I can picture it so clearly . . . All his works fascinate me. He has such an understanding outlook on life, such an insight into people's thoughts . . . The Caine Mutiny is practically required reading for all Naval officers. It is, by the way, a very good description of much of the life in the Navy. Every one of us feels like a chapter out of Caine Mutiny at one time or another, and often, too. Sometimes it really is that bad.*

At the end of this letter, Dave tells her "she's everything." Sometime during this eight-month period of furtive letter writing, he wonders if he can tell her that he loves her. He decides it's not too soon.

But inevitably, the pang of their long distance relationship is too much of a burden. Dave is now off his ship, stationed in Germany. Either because he's met someone else, or he simply realizes the futility of writing love letters to someone he barely knows, he wisely and kindly ends it. He begs her to understand. "We were not together enough to really get to know each other," he writes. *For some time, the memory of your beauty haunted me, but now I want to make a clean break of it and write "Finis" to a wonderful chapter of my life. Will you please send me the letter I gave you on the ship? The one that began such a wonderful dream for us. Please write me, Mim, and tell me that you do understand and that I'm not as big a heel as I am. Yours with love, Mim. Dave.*

She does write to him. I have her rough drafted letter. I don't know if she was heart broken or not, but she says, ". . . I do honestly and truly understand how you feel." Perhaps she felt the same, coming home from her secretarial job to Winans Avenue and receiving yet another passionate letter from someone she didn't really know very well. Maybe they were exciting, and maybe she did feel some love toward him, but she may have also sensed something false in such passion. Maybe his loneliness spurred him on.

It's possible Dave's letters gave her something else, too, besides making her feel sexy and attractive and wanted. Maybe through his letters from abroad, she starts to wonder what it would be like for *her* to travel; his letters may have been the spring board for making her feel more awake to the world beyond New Jersey.

Her ambitions start to grow further than what she wanted as a young girl, to be a receptionist and sit behind a desk all day. There is a whole, big wide world out there! Other young women whom she knew had the goal of finding a husband. They did not think beyond the boundaries of Cranford and they did not have that ambition to leave. Not Mim.

She was compelled to leave her hometown. My mother knew there was more outside of Cranford to discover, partly through Dave's letters, and also through books. She certainly saw New

York City. She recalls taking her younger brothers into the city and walking around the Village. She remembers Jonathon in particular being fascinated by the automats where you could put in a coin, open a little window, and take out a sandwich! She saved her money from her secretarial job, which afforded her to see plays and experience the thrill of Broadway. She saw movies and she romanticized about the sunshine out west.

Then she made up her mind. She thought her friends Joanne and Elaine would come with her, but they both backed out, and in the end, my mom boarded a plane to California alone. It was the mid-1950s. As a young woman leaving her hometown, she demonstrated in her early 20s a spirit of unusual independence. She found she had wings.

Her younger sister was inconsolable over Mim's departure. My mother always had a special place in her heart for Annie. She still does. My Aunt Ann recalls sitting on the edge of the tub, sobbing and sobbing when Mim told her she was leaving. She was 14 years younger than Mim and her big sister was like a mother to her. Mim looked out for her in the turbulence of their home and now that safety net would be gone, but never the love. Their bond lasted a lifetime.

Miriam knew that she had to leave New Jersey and in doing so, she set out to find the most glamorous place she could think of. Where else but Los Angeles? Although she didn't want to stay in Cranford just looking around for a husband, she did have her heart set on finding someone to marry eventually. She hoped to meet someone on the other side of the country. Right away she found a job in Beverly Hills working in a real-estate office in the escrow department. It's possible this is where she first acquired a sense of finance. At an early age, my mother learned the importance of saving and investing her earnings.

She rented a room in a house in Beverly Hills, and had a few encounters with some Hollywood legends, too. Ray Bolger, the actor who played the scarecrow in *The Wizard of Oz*, was a neighbor. Jimmy Stewart attended the same church as my mother. She had the cheek to ask him for a light of her cigarette once. She tells me this now and laughs and says, "But he wouldn't go out on a date with me."

In reality, the only man she had her heart set on was Norman. Looking around for romance, she joined a singles group in her neighborhood Presbyterian Church, and that's where she met her first, true love. He was from a wealthy family and lived in the same neighborhood as she did in Beverly Hills.

It was the closest relationship she'd ever had with anyone to date, and she says their time together was intensely emotional. Norman loved the outdoors. The letters he wrote to her reflect this. My mother saved everything, including stacks and stacks of letters from Norman declaring his love for her, and for God. They are tediously religious. He encloses long prayers that he's written for her and in every letter he talks about God and "Christ our Savior" and "His glory." He wasn't an academic, nor was he a writer. But he was tender and kind, and he and my mother were great companions. They even took a camping trip by themselves once, and there's a photo of my mother wearing shorts and a short-sleeved, checkered blouse sitting cross-legged on a picnic blanket in the woods smiling up at him, their camping gear spread about. I wonder about their sleeping arrangements. I ask my mom, but she either doesn't remember or she won't say.

I also asked her under what circumstances she washed her hair at Norman's house once, but she doesn't remember that either. She only remembers coming down to the dinner table with rollers in her hair. Well, what else is a girl from Jersey to do with wet hair? The last thing my mother knew about was formality, so why wouldn't she come to the table with rollers in her hair? She remembers Norman's sister being angry. If they were of a certain class, living in an elegant home, it's not hard to imagine the sister being affronted by this young woman showing up at the dinner table looking so inappropriate.

She may have lived in Hollywood, but my mother did not easily shed her poor Jersey roots, and was often surprised by anything that was a notch above those roots. It hadn't been that long before when she was at the home of her friend, Elaine, in New Jersey, when Elaine's mother presented Mim with a sectioned grapefruit. Never in her life had she had a piece of fruit that was so perfectly prepared that each and every section could be eaten individually. She was awed by the elegant simplicity of it. My mother's introduction to a life she'd never experienced in her own upbringing was in the presentation of that sectioned grapefruit on a doily. She never forgot the impression that made on her and in years to come, when preparing food and entertaining, presentation was paramount.

I do wonder if class played into Norman's unwillingness to marry my mother. "I hadn't loved anyone before that, but he didn't want to marry, so he broke it off, even though he loved me," she says of him. He was a soulful man, and it's possible that class had nothing to do with it; rather, marriage was just not for him. Or his family persuaded him to avoid the girl from Jersey.

Still, that year in California was one of the best years of her life. Her church group voted her secretary. She made friends right away and felt accepted and well liked. They planned social gatherings, city outings, weekend camping trips, day trips to the beach, in between singing songs, and oh yeah—worshiping.

After one year, it was time to return home, to see her parents and her younger siblings, to reassess her life. Little did she know that when she got back to Cranford, her friend Elaine would be waiting on Mim's doorstep, practically begging her to take her to California.

Chapter Five

⌒

The carefree, "California or Bust" days that my mom and her life-long friend, Elaine, spent together in their early twenties became a legend in our household and a longed-for memory, which she recounted to us, her children, so many times. I think that by talking about the experiences that she had with Elaine, driving across country—from New Jersey to California—she hoped that we, too, would get a chance in our lifetime to experience the freedom, the escapades, the shenanigans, the *fun* that she and Elaine had together making their way west. They took to that road like it was nobody's business, and I bet they didn't have a map. I imagine them pulling out of Cranford, pulling away from the mechanic who told them that their car wouldn't make it out of town, and asking him anyway how to get to California.

Having a friend the second time around made it a different kind of journey than her first trip west. They had nowhere to be. They were in no rush. They were able to take their time and follow whichever path they desired, whichever way the wind took them.

In writing about this story now, years after I'd heard the details of that trip, I questioned my mother for more. I sat on the couch with her in our apartment in Dhaka. But she'd respond to my questions by saying, "That's a *good* question," without providing an answer. She couldn't remember how old she was or what year they left.

Then it suddenly occurred to me that I could just ask Elaine! With my mom sitting next to me, I picked up my laptop and dashed off an email. The very next morning little gems of details, long forgotten by my mom, sprang out of the treasure chest of Elaine's reply. Elaine got out a map of the United States and the memories came rushing in. It was 1956, so my mom was 22. They packed their luggage, and jammed a full-sized ironing board in the car with them. This was the days before wash and wear, and to leave the house with wrinkles? I mean, really. The ironing board doubled as a tabletop in the backseat for which to prepare lunch. Elaine drove; my mom made the peanut butter and jelly sandwiches.

They left Jersey right after the Christmas holidays in Elaine's 1950 Ford. They drove south to say goodbye to Elaine's father who was working on a highway job. They were in such a hurry that they got pulled over by a state trooper and couldn't talk him out of a ticket—the only ticket they got on their journey. They stayed with Elaine's relatives in Missouri—but Elaine can tell the rest better than I can.

When my Missouri relatives learned that we planned to drive straight west to reach California, they told us we couldn't do that in the middle of winter because there were high mountains and the roads might be closed. I doubt that we had even looked at the map before then. With that discouraging news, we decided that we had better head south, so next morning we did. We saw the Hot Springs Nat'l Park in Arkansas on the map, so we headed there. There were public baths there and they took us one at a time and each of us had a different person to guide us through the series of baths and steam rooms, ending in a massage room. Mim was just ahead of me and as we passed, she told me to be sure to ask for the massage, which of course, I did. She didn't tell me that the massage was actually a form of torture and that I would be pummeled until I pleaded for mercy. We were so weakened and exhausted after the baths that we could only drive four miles out of town and had to find a motel even though it was the middle of the afternoon and we had planned to drive another hundred miles.

How they ended up in New Orleans after that was, according to my mom, because of a notice they saw on a library bulletin board for Mardi Gras. They must have looked at each other at the same time, simultaneously nodded and said, "Guess where we're going? What are we waiting for? Let's *goooooo!!!*"

Elaine's email provides another missing link:

So we landed in a big city without a place to stay. We were having trouble finding a place to stay so I stopped the car in front of a nice looking building and told Mim, "Go see if they have a room." She went up to the rather luxurious looking home and asked for a room.

I remember the next thing that was said to my mom because I'd heard that line so many times, but I couldn't put it into context. Who said it to her? When did that happen? I finally had my answer. The man who answered the door looked at my mom and said to her, "Ma'am, this is a *funeral* parlor."

When you're in New Orleans and Mardi Gras is only eight weeks away and you're in your twenties and you have nowhere else to be anyway, the temptation to just hang around until party time must be great. And it was. The temptation was just too great. They rented rooms. But to afford the stopover, they needed jobs. As Elaine points out in her correspondence to me, back then all you really needed to do was dress up, walk in for an interview, and start the job the next day. Good thing they had that ironing board.

Two tall, attractive women, one blond, the other brunette, walked into the office of the president of Tulane University, and landed jobs. Of course they didn't tell the truth about how long they were staying in New Orleans, or else they wouldn't have been hired. It's a testament to Elaine's character that she says that lie still haunts her. It definitely doesn't haunt my mom—a fact that is perhaps a testament to *her* character, too. My mother has always had a bit of the daredevil in her. Elaine writes,

Mim had worked at Standard Oil in N. J. and was an excellent stenographer. I had been to a secretarial school in Rhode Island and had had a few office jobs in N. J. but I wasn't a very good stenographer . . . I told Mim we should get jobs at a college because working on a college campus was fun and there was no pressure as there was in corporate business offices . . . The office was one big open room with desks all around the perimeter (no cubbies) . . . I could look across this big open room and see Mim with stacks of paper on her desk, typing away as fast as she could all day long. Her boss was a big fundraiser and a very ambitious college president. My boss was a vice president with a law practice on the side and he was out of the office more than he was in it . . . Since he was seldom there, I had little work to do, so I would be sitting at my desk filing my nails and looking across at Mim working harder than she had ever worked before. At the end of the day, she would remind me that I had told her how easy college jobs were.

What my mom remembers, to this day, is flirting with the men in that office who had girlfriends already, but oh well. She remembers the French Quarter and exploring the streets and the drinking and the glorious fun. Elaine remembers the *beignets*, the hot, fried doughnuts covered in powdered sugar. She tried to get the recipe but the cook told her it's such a secret that even *he* didn't have the recipe. Bags of ingredients were delivered to him and he was only told the proportions to use. "So we never got the recipe," she says. "Years later Mim sent me a paperback cookbook with that recipe in it. I guess it was no longer secret." Elaine continues in her email to me,

We did splurge a few times. One time we went to Commander's Palace and another time to Antoine's. I'm ashamed to say we stole a white cloth napkin from each place, but I never used mine because they had the name of the restaurant embroidered on them and I was too embarrassed to use them. My sins still haunt me.

No doubt it was my mother who was behind the scheme of taking the napkins. When you don't really feel guilty about something, you tend to forget it. And I'd never heard about those napkins until I heard about it from Elaine, 60 years after the fact.

Marry Me Stop

They stayed through Mardi Gras to see the floats, the flamboyant cross-dressers in their make-up and high heels, the beads tossed into the crowd. It was thrilling and wild and I imagine they got caught up in the hype and jazz and stimulation that only a party like Mardi Gras can offer where, as Elaine says, "everybody was your friend." They had a ball. But the party was well over by now and it was time to continue west, and push on with their goal.

The whole long time that my mother was away from California, Norman longed for his Miriam to return to him. In New Orleans a letter manages to reach her, despite his uncertainty of Mim's whereabouts. *". . . Now then, as for you: where are you? How are you? When are you coming back? I am anxious to meet Elaine as you have told me what a fine person she is and I pray that the Savior will or has worked wonders for her and that she may see His glory and believe."* It must have been confusing to her, his loving her but not wanting to marry. He wanted a girlfriend, not a wife. But she did not let the feelings she had for him stop her from enjoying life and being fully present with her friend.

She was also prepared, on her trip with Elaine, to take advantage of her surroundings. Outside of San Antonio in a little town called Bandera there was a saloon, the perfect place to sashay on in and ask if anyone knows of a dude ranch where they could stay. Of *course* they wanted to stay on a dude ranch. They were in *Texas!* Word got passed around the dance hall that two attractive women from out east were looking for a dude ranch. It probably wasn't hard, from there on out, to procure one. "Benny over there has a dude ranch," someone said. Of course he did. "Follow me," Benny said.

He hopped in his truck and they followed in their car. It was night and they really didn't know where the heck they were going, but they drove and drove, down dusty, unpaved roads until they arrived at the "dude ranch" where the only dude in sight was Benny. He showed them a room and when they closed the door, a woman's bathrobe was hanging on the back of it. What have we gotten ourselves into, my mother remembers saying to Elaine in a hushed whisper. They quickly pushed a dresser in front of the door before turning out the lights for the night. It could have been a dude ranch, but it wasn't what they were expecting. In the morning a cook made breakfast and Benny showed off his horses. And then they high-tailed it outta there.

They dragged themselves out of their motel in Arizona early one morning to see the Painted Desert. Nothing spectacular there. Maybe it was the wrong time of day, or a cloudy day. They finally entered California at Needles on Route 66. A terrific sandstorm was in full swing; even still, the officer at the checkpoint looked in their trunk for contraband. The sand from the storm tore a strip of paint right off the car.

It was a good thing my mother made such good friends in Beverly Hills the year before because it was easy for the two—weary by now—travelers to find a place to crash. The obvious choice was Norman. Elaine must have been surprised by the "gorgeous hilltop mansion," as she describes Norman's home, and the live-in help and the stables and horses. But Beverly Hills was not where Elaine wanted to stay, so out popped the map and a pen and they circled all the places they knew of that had community colleges. They both agreed it was time to get serious.

Monterey sounded great, and they were delighted when they arrived. But what about San Francisco? They kept driving north to explore the city, and then headed right back to Monterey. That was their place. They found a duplex at the foot of the hills below Monterey Peninsula College. They could walk to classes and into town. It was perfect.

Two years after meeting Miriam, Norman is still writing passionate letters to her. In 1958 he writes a long letter while on a journey, by flight, "over some of the wildest areas in the U.S. and Canada." From Baffin Island, Canada, in June of 1958 he writes,

Miriam, I want to tell you how very much your wonderful letter means to me. I missed you even before you left and ever since. When your letter arrived I rushed to read it and I felt my emotions welling up within me and I choked, then cried then read it again. I have it with me now as I want to read it again. I am glad that you have been enjoying yourself and only wish that I was with you or you with me as I know that we would have much fun together and as always we would enjoy each others company so much. Life is a strange thing and I am a strange thing also. I miss you very much as I always have when we are far apart. I knew that I would love you and miss you but I cannot claim you as my own though I would very much like to.

Why he cannot claim her as his own is uncertain. It seems he's made his decision not to marry, despite his deep feelings and great love.

Norm came up to Monterey for visits, presenting Miriam with beautiful and expensive gifts, jewelry and cashmere sweaters. He was in love with her and she with him. And that was enough of a reason for my mother to eventually move back down to Beverly Hills. Did she just love him for the gifts he brought? He hinted at it, and asked her if it was so. Elaine remembers Mim confiding in her over this. But Mim's response to Norm was that of course I love you for the gifts you bring, but I also love you for yourself just as much. Elaine somehow learned that Norm's mother told him that Mim is just after him for his money. It sounds like Norm's family was not a good match for my mother. Maybe my mom sensed trouble ahead and his not wanting to marry was a good thing, even though she may have still been conflicted at the time. It was time to leave Beverly Hills for good. The following fall, both women met up again in Berkeley. That was their new home.

As my mom and I walk through the park in Dhaka, we are talking about this adventure of hers. Her shoulders are very stooped now. She kind of leans forward when she walks and I have to remind her to swing her arms and lift her head. But at 79-years-old she still has a song in her heart for the time she had with Elaine. She lifts her head now and looks at me with a laugh and sings the first line of the old classic, "Cal-i-forn-ia, here we come!"

Chapter Six

My mother's life reads like a checklist of good choices. Finish high school, check. Go to California, check. Become a resident of the state of California, check. She and Elaine were now enrolled in UC Berkeley and as residents of the state of California, they would get a bachelor's degree practically for free. My mom scored another good deal by getting free rent in an apartment above a garage in exchange for taking care of the children of a wealthy family. As for Elaine, she was soon to meet her future husband and begin a family of her own.

Should Miriam have talked with the man on the bus who was wearing a wedding ring? Could that be added to her checklist of good choices? After all, it was safe. He was married. What could happen? Their conversation was lively, even though short. They were only going from San Francisco to Berkeley. She told him where she was from. Coincidentally, he was from New York! I like to think that it *was* a good choice, or else, well—where in this story would *I* have fit in?

Months later she was walking down a hill rushing to get to her classes and the man with whom she'd had that nice conversation on the bus was walking up it. He stopped walking, looked at her and said, "New Jersey." I can see it as I write it, that initial attraction in his eyes that my father had for my mother. He was no longer wearing that wedding ring either.

They saw each other again at the library, near an apartment he was now living in alone. At what point he told her he had three teenage children, I don't know. It must have been obvious how much older he was than she. What she didn't know at the time was that it was the same as the age difference between her own parents, 18 years. But she accepted his invitation to his apartment for dinner anyway. "I was so innocent," she now says. "To think I'd go over to a man's apartment alone. I was adventuresome, but I was innocent."

Chopped chicken liver and slices of bread were on the table and my mom thought, Oh, that's nice—open-faced sandwiches. She didn't realize he'd made the main dish and that it was in the kitchen—Sole *Fouquet*. This is probably where he declared that infamous line of his: If you can read you can cook. My dad sure could read, but cook? Still, I'm impressed with his menu, and so was she.

Somewhere in between library shelves, the college campus, and his apartment, she fell in love with Ronald, who was divorced by now. She admired him for his intellect; he was the most well-read, intelligent man she'd ever known. He had things about life to teach her and she was an ingénue, captivated by his intellectual power.

Marry Me Stop

To him she was always Miriam, never Mim. He had his M.A. in library science (and later in political science) and worked as a librarian in the Adult Education Department in the Oakland Public Library.

Part of my father's job at the library was to moderate a program on public television, out of KQED. The show was called "Current Issue." He was televised holding a round table discussion with popular actors, writers, psychiatrists, professors, and politicians about the issues of the day. A review of the show that appeared in February 1958 calls "Current Issue" the best program on T.V.: "If Current Issue is somewhat like betting on the ponies—hoping a good argument will develop—it is at least the best race available each week on San Francisco television."

My father moderated it for a year, then hired another man to moderate it while he produced it, choosing the articles for discussion and the people who would appear on the air. Sadly, that race ended when the funds ran dry. And my father found himself out of a job.

He must have been pretty desperate when he took a job as a taxicab driver. I don't know how long that job lasted, but it could have ended when his brakes failed at the top of one of those famous San Francisco hills. His instincts were sharp enough for him to turn the wheel into the side of the road, knocking down an electric pole in the process. The taxicab flipped over, but he got out with barely a scratch. The only other damage I know of was that all of the lights in my mother's neighborhood went out.

My mother may not have been too concerned at this stage in their relationship about his employment prospects. She loved him and he made her laugh. Standing outside of a movie theatre, waiting for him to buy the tickets, she was unaware that he asked for one adult ticket and one child. Why the person in the ticket booth didn't question my father about the tall blond behind him who clearly wasn't a child, I don't know. Maybe he, too, was charmed by my father's confidence. He could get away with stuff like that. He had that cheek, and that combination of smart, serious, and very witty.

Miriam had about four years in California, and a few romances under her slim-fitting belt before she met my father. One romance in particular was a hard one to let go, and that was with Norman. It was tough. When she met my father, Norman wasn't quite a thing of the past just yet.

My mother received letters around the same time from both men. If she was weighing whom to choose based on the missives she received, Norman could not carry his weight in words. There was nothing to compare. My father was a *man* of letters. He was a writer and words were his art. If my father hoped to weigh in on his love for her and persuade her not to stick with the other guy, all he really needed to do was sharpen his pencil.

Both men loved her; neither wanted to marry. Norman was adamant that marriage was not for him. She remembers a phone call with him where he made this perfectly clear. They finally ended their relationship; my mom realized it was over for good.

Marry Me Stop

While continuing to take classes at Berkeley, Miriam's relationship with Ronald developed. She was even introduced to his three children. But for him, it must have seemed like just yesterday when he'd left a troubled marriage. He could not have been too eager to enter into another marriage so soon after his last one ended. He made it clear—it just wasn't going to happen.

Chapter Seven

Fine, then. She had her degree in Childhood Development and Psychology. She was independent and she always found a way of taking care of herself. But there was no way Miriam was going to be jilted a second time by another man who loved her but wouldn't marry her—and just stick around to be reminded of that daily. Her answer this time was to go home. She said good-bye to Ronald and flew back to New Jersey where for one year she taught elementary school.

She had long conversations on the phone with Ronald. His eldest daughter was in the process of moving east, to live with a family friend in Massachusetts whom my father knew from Berkeley. On the phone, they arranged for Raissa to meet Miriam in New York City. Raissa recalls the two of them having the time of their lives together. They saw Mary Martin in "The Sound of Music" on Broadway. "Third row, center. Daddy's 18th birthday present to me," Raissa says. Even I remember hearing stories of how she and my mother clutched hands, three rows from the stage, just barely containing themselves with the thrill of it all, their hearts practically stopping at Mary Martin's high notes.

Despite their continued bond and her growing fondness of Ronald's children, he was still unprepared for the responsibilities of a new marriage. So the only thing that made sense to my mother at that time was to take her broken heart on a ship and head to Europe. She packed some nice clothes in her suitcase in the fall of '62, got on that ship, and a few weeks later, disembarked in Holland. By train, she took her time traveling, stopping in Switzerland, and then Venice, and kept going south.

The first letter that I found from my father written to my mother during her time of wanderlust was written in September. My father is house hunting and job hunting, and missing Miriam terribly. He wants to write to her while she's abroad, but he's not sure where to send a letter.

Dearest, dearest Miriam,

To begin from the beginning. You are missed. I would have written sooner, but I've been so harried that I haven't been thinking with my usual wonted keenness. I've been waiting to hear from you to have an address to write to. Tim [her brother] *came into library the night before last and said he had written you.—But where will you send it if Miriam hasn't written you yet?—c/o American Express, Vienna. But of course!*

Thereafter, whatever town she happened to arrive in, she continued to go straight to the American Express office to check her mail, a service provided to Americans traveling overseas.

The stresses of the world are on my father's shoulders in this letter: looking for a new place to live, trying to sell some furniture, making stabs at the book he's writing, feeling disappointment with his job, and now this:

Headache No. Four, he writes. *I got ticket coming home from San Mateo for passing stop sign. Just what was needed.*

He speaks disparagingly about his job. *Foothill College is—not to put too fine a point on the matter—a high class department store pretending to be an institution for higher learning. The Dress Code is the Bible of the place. New instructors warned at first meeting that they must never, never be seen without a jacket on. No Nobel laureates in sweat shirts allowed. The* spirit *of the place isn't right . . .*

The following month I'm happy to read that he is in better spirits. He's finally found a place to live in Los Altos.

October 1962:

I have never lived in a place that I like better than my little cottage here.

Other areas of his life are also looking up.

The job at Foothill is O.K. No problems there. I have not yet received a full month's pay, so I'm not sure I can live on my salary. But I think I should be able to . . .

And this:

The VW is working beautifully. It is just like my little cottage. Both compact, wholly adequate, all that is necessary for both to be. They even match in color!

And she wrote to him, but my father—unlike my mother—kept practically nothing. I only have two letters she wrote to him during that time, but they hadn't been written yet at this point in her trip. In a letter written in October, my father refers to a letter she wrote to him in response to his letter that reached her in Vienna.

"*. . . You write beautiful letters, Miriam. Not a phony word in them. They are like the way you read—simple, clear, beautiful. They are like you. I have your Vienna letter in front of me. Yes, Miriam dear, we would have been a good couple. I know this. You have only given good things to me. Whatever I said in the emotion of the moment about "destroying me," or harming me in any way, was never meant to refer to the quality of your love, which is as good and tender as you are yourself, but simply to what I felt—and still feel—is my own incapacity at this time to take on all of the responsibilities of family life . . .*"

Miriam kept going south.

Italy! She no longer cared so much about why she was running away. She was in Florence, one of the most beautiful cities in the world and she was going to do and see all that was available and affordable to her: the art galleries, the meandering side streets, the courtyards and fountains, the opera house. She fell in love again, this time with a city where beauty was around every corner and in every stone statue and where she couldn't have felt farther away from her New Jersey roots. Botticelli's naked, female forms mesmerized her. And what could be more beautiful than the setting sun behind the *Duomo,* the cathedral in the center of the city with its magnificent red dome?

I've heard my mother gush about her time in Italy over and over again. It was a place that she let herself escape into. It was the first time in her life where she saw art, really saw it. She didn't need to have studied it or read books about the history of art or even understood what she was really looking at to appreciate Michelangelo, Leonardo De Vinci, Donatello. She just did. She appreciated it on her own, without the need of a guide to tell her how to appreciate it, or what she should know before looking at it. She wandered to her heart's content absorbing this lush, new landscape of the world of art.

I think about my mother, wandering alone in a foreign city, without inhibitions. I see a young and attractive woman, holding herself tall, walking with a purpose, climbing the steps of the museum curious about what she will find inside. Consulting her map. Swinging her handbag. Shading her eyes in a sun-filled square. Leaning against a stone pillar. Talking to strangers with a friendly, all-American forthright manner.

She is friendly still. She's lost a bit of her swing, but she has not lost that smile and she has not lost her sense of fun. Most people I've met on this journey with my mother have welcomed and embraced her. When others laugh at her jokes, I am better able to accept her presence at my side and the decision that we've made of having her live with us. They are welcoming her, and at the same time, supporting me.

Take, for example, two friends I've made in Dhaka. I was with them not long ago when we sat down at the small table and each ordered a drink. I'd just taken them on a walk by Gulshan Lake, an area in Dhaka they'd not been to before. We ended up at Mango, a café hidden in an upstairs room, down an alleyway, away from the noisy street. I stumbled upon it one day by noticing the sign hanging above an archway and wanted to bring my new friends.

Marry Me Stop

During the chit-chatting, I thought about my mom and wondered what she was doing. She'd like this coffee shop. She'd want a cappuccino. It suddenly felt wrong, not having her here with us. She was at home, alone with the housekeeper; she'd have woken up and wondered where I was. She was probably pacing. And it would be so easy to get her here. "Would you mind if I asked my mom to join us?" I asked my friends, interrupting the flow of conversation. Their response was the type of kindness that continues to surprise me. My friends both immediately urged me to call my driver to pick her up. One of the perks of being in Dhaka is that hiring a driver is highly recommended and encouraged, and ours was becoming indispensible, especially in moments like these when he could so quickly assist my mother.

Sitting at our little table inside the café, my mother, who was now happily sipping a cappuccino, asked one of my friends where her favorite place to travel is. My friend talked about Italy. How one day she and her husband want to buy property there. I could tell my mother wanted to talk. "How 'bout you?" she asked my mom. Again, a kindness. An interest in her and her life. "Well, Italy," my mom said. I saw the story coming from a mile away.

Their eyes don't glaze over. They lean forward as my mom transports them to Florence and the opera house and the night she'd met a wonderful guy. She was alone and tall and blond, well dressed and gorgeous. That description is never part of her story, but I imagine that she was. She had red lipstick, no doubt, and a bright smile, but she wasn't naïve. She carried her common sense with her to Europe, and the night she was offered a seat at the opera house by a handsome Italian man because she had standing-room-only tickets, she politely refused. But the man insisted and in the end she accepted. However, she could not accept the offer a second time, after intermission when this kind man again insisted that she take his seat; plus, the seat that he urged her to sit in had flipped back up, without his knowledge.

As he tried to push her into his seat, he was unaware that he was really pushing her on to the floor, so my mother lost her composure and started to laugh. The silliness of it all made her laugh harder, not able to get the words out of her mouth to tell him that the chair had flipped back up, as he continued to gently push her to the ground.

My friends laugh and laugh at this story, and even though I've heard it a million times, I laugh, too. I'm proud of how well she's told it; she didn't leave anything out, and she had her timing down. She says at the end of the story that they had a wonderful evening together following the opera, going out to dinner together with his friends afterwards, even though she wistfully says that she never saw him again. The very next day, he left Italy for Africa.

She travelled south to Rome, Naples and Pompeii where she bought a small fresco of the head of a woman that she had hanging on her bedroom wall for years.

But my father catches up to her.

November 1962:

" . . . And those Italians you teach English to? And all those other wily, up-to-no-gooders you are meeting and sipping wine with in sunny and song-filled piazzas? You must be very careful, Miriam sweetheart. Think. I have met European men and I know whereof I speak. They are like all men. (C'mere.) The sooner you get back to me and Old Glory the better. Talitha was with me over last weekend.

Marry Me Stop

She wants to live with me—loves my little cottage—but I don't think it best, at this time, anyway. She told me she loves you. I thought Kennedy handled Cuba crisis very well. Good man, JFK. Tali and I agree on everything. Write me. Ronald.

Miriam eventually crossed the channel to England—where she fell in love with a place all over again and became an instant Anglophile.

And England fell in love with her—or at least one family in particular did. It was the holidays and my mom, alone and in need of a place to stay and in need of a purpose, responded to a notice she spotted on a bulletin board requesting the services of a nanny. She dialed the number and the first eager words she said to the woman with the British accent on the other end were, "Do you need any help?"

There was a pause on the other end—an astonished silence at my mother's good timing, "When can you come?" Fifteen priests were about to arrive on Priscilla's doorstep for lunch and she desperately needed help, not just that day but for all of the holidays. "Tonight," my mother cheerfully responded, and she got on a train and boldly made her way south to Canterbury to live with a family in "The Vicarage."

That family was the Verneys and they took my mother in and she was cared for and admired, and made to feel almost instantly like part of the family. Steven Verney was a minister and about fifteen years after my mother lived with him and his wife Priscilla and their four children, Steven Verney became a bishop—the Bishop of Repton, in a village in Derbyshire, England. She stayed in touch with this kind family for more than 20 years. I eventually got to meet them when I was a young adult traveling in England.

Regina Landor

Letters poured in to The Vicarage from Ronald to Miriam.
December 27:

My dearest Miriam,

You are such an upsetting person to me—so very, very upsetting. I received your letter, written a week ago, just 5 minutes ago, read it, and had to reach at once for a pen to answer you. How tempting you are to me. That's not a "nice" way of putting it, but it is candid. I respond to your spirit and to the expression of your likes and dislikes, your values—in a one-to-one correspondence. I can only say, that when you are you, in the environment in which you find yourself at home, at peace, even if only for a moment, you are beautiful to me, and the thought of you beautiful. I only read your letter once before moving to answer it; I shall read it many times over. But in my hasty first reading, I thought, how right that you should have found "The Vicarage"—but not how lucky. Because it was not simply luck. You answered the notice. You acted. You took the chance. You dared to love what you did not see—and lo, it was love. You are such a good sweet dear loving beautiful person. That's what I think of you.

What also stands out, in addition to Ronald's admiration of her, is that my mother told him about a meeting she had in London with Norman. Even today my mother remembers the shock she experienced at bumping into him at a train station. It must have been during one of his many excursions. I wonder if my mother is purposefully torturing my father by telling him about Norman, and about the Italian men she met, and about the eligible, young men that the Verneys by now are trying to set her up with.

Now I've re-read your letter and see things I missed in hasty 1ˢᵗ reading. That 4 hour lunch with Norm. How long is he going to

50

be there? (In England). I think it's ridiculous, absolutely ree-dick-u-lous. (In the middle of last sentence, I just had an idea. Am going to phone you tonight at the Vicarage. Tried to call just now but all circuits busy . . .)

About "Norman, my dear friend." . . . Your letter pleads for an end to ambiguity . . . England—and especially where you are—sounds like a place we should be together. You are precious to me. That's all I can say. Your letters are treasured. Just a line from you means much. Remember this. Much love, Miriam darling. Ronald

My mom had been corresponding with Norman for about six years now. My father is right. Let go already!

Whether or not my mother had a hidden scheme, the letters from my father start to heat up. If she had a plan of becoming his wife by letting him know about the other men around her, it's working.

28 Dec 1962

Miriam dearest,

You see, across mountains, deserts, oceans, and financial insolvency, I reach out to you. Not bad, eh? As you say, "I'm not so unusual, Ronald." How true. And yet—yet—there must be something there to motivate me. What could it be? Whatever it is, I miss it when it's not here comforting and delighting me.

Toward the end of the same letter, he writes:

You say to me: What do you <u>want</u>, Ronald? Either marry me or forget me (you say). But I can't do either. I can only live one life at a time, and the life I am living now is not compatible with the responsibilities of marriage . . . But if you ask me what I <u>want</u>, I can say I wish you were near me; that I could see you often; that we could be together as much as possible. You need hardly tell me that this is not what you *want; that this is not fair to you; that you want marriage—the whole bit or nothing. I know. I can think of you only with love. Ronald.*

At some point during these ardent epistles that flew back and forth across the ocean, she asked my father not to write her anymore. It was too painful—being in love but being denied the opportunity of marriage.

My father ignores that request.

31 Dec 1962

Miriam dear,

All I ask is, Do not (repeat, do not) fall in love with anyone else until you see me first. Your letter of 27 Dec just arrived. Usual rite here. Keep looking out window for mail truck. It arrives. Dash out. Beautiful red, white, & blue bordered envelope. Tremendous surge of patriotism. Tear open envelope. Feverish reading—well, hasty, anyway. Minute of reflection (aided by cup of tea & piece of fruit cake.) Reach for pen. Here I am. I love you. Now, to answer parts of your letter specifically. First thing I remember (without looking at letter) is comment of your sister-in-law, that she feels more sorry for me than for you (on your return from Calif.) Wise woman. I agree. Problem is me, not you. Because you are a gem, a beauty, a treasure, a love. You are all that any woman has to be, and that is much. Your letters go straight, straight, to their mark, and that is me, and I can squirm little under their penetration . . . (Parenthesis: Your attention and letters to Blake, Raissa, Talitha have meant much to me, not to say to them also . . . You have become precious to them, too, Miriam.)

Sometime between January 7 and January 11 my father has a complete change of heart on the matter of remarrying.

7 Jan 1963

Marry Me Stop

. . . I began the preceding paragraph because I didn't know how else to get into this letter except by saying something factual. But I am far from feeling factual or prosaic. I can imagine that my letters to you in recent days have disturbed you—perhaps even been cruel. But I did not write as I did except out of my own deep perplexity. Well, the time is over for that.

He does not ask her to marry him just yet. But definitely hints at it in that last sentence. He ends his letter by saying,

. . . What I really want to say in writing this letter, is that I miss you and wish you were here now. If you are coming, I hope it will be soon. I feel tired now—and sore. Your presence would be a balm.

Finally, finally it arrives. A thin, typed-written envelope is delivered to her at The Vicarage from Western Union. It's a telegram and between the spelled-out punctuation are the words Miriam has yearned for: "COME HOME STOP MARRY ME STOP"

The children she is looking after are enchanted—their American nanny is getting married! They dance around her and take a curtain ring and put it on her finger. Miriam is going home. She is going to be a bride at last!

In what appears to be the very next form of communication from my father, he writes,

It's not getting married that I mind so much as it is the awful cable and telephone charges. There should be a law that the wives, sweethearts, children and other beloved characters should not be allowed to travel beyond a certain distance from the man who loves them if he is poor (or sumpin' like dat). Raissa called yesterday (collect) from Amherst because she was feeling a little blue. Bang! There went sirloin steak for the next three months. And you—what about you? You're just as bad. England, yet! Cheaper to keep you near me. I mentioned to Raissa that I had popped the question, but that as yet I had had no reply. You have endeared yourself to the three Landor poppets.

At last, in all of my mother's papers and photos, there appears a letter from her. My father must have saved it, and she put it in her own stack of keepsakes. It's from January 11.

Dearest Ronald,

Last evening it was impossible to sleep after your call. This morning at 5:30 wanted to get up, but rested until 6:30 then got ready to leave for a day in London to make arrangements for leaving.

She talks about how fond she's become of the Verneys. "... *tonight when I came home the four children threw themselves in my arms. It's going to be difficult leaving them.*"

She is still a little confused at how quickly the turn of events happened. But she takes comfort in her own words: "*Everything will be alright when I'm in your arms again,*" she writes.

She discusses taking a ship back to America. The next ship departs January 16th. But she's eager to return and she also wants to see her family before going to California. At the end of her letter she writes, *Ronald, May be radical change in plans. Will let you know immediately!*

The change in plans is that she rushes into a travel agency in London and secures the very last seat on a plane leaving for New York.

It's a good thing. My father writes that he's not a fan of long engagements; even though he expresses regret at thinking he may be terminating her England trip prematurely.

A letter that's waiting for her on her return to America is dated 17 January.

Marry Me Stop

Miriam darling,

I'm so glad you decided to fly back instead of waiting for that slow old boat. If the ways in which you gratify me before marriage are any index of what awaits me after, all I can say is, It's all highly suspicious.

I had intended to call you last night because I thought you might have felt that my letter to you yesterday was too much taken up with "things", that I had not sent you the "assurance" you had asked for—you know, my usual irrepressible flippancy. But, then, you know me by now and I must trust that you do, and there is no time like now for trust to begin.

You left England before my last letter to you there arrived. Perhaps it has been forwarded to you by now. In it I said—I repeat—I know I am getting the right woman for me. I could not, would not, say Yes except unreservedly. You were so good in staying with me as you did. I needed this, and you were there for me, in every way. I know that I took an unconscionably long way around, but there was no short cut. You understood—your love understood, and knew better for us than I knew, perhaps even better than you yourself could know. I believe that with God's help, Miriam dear, you will have in me a husband, as I know I have in you a wife. We will help each other; for we both want, above all, to be good children of God. How good it is that we should both have the same vision of life!

I expect you early next week, so won't write again. I love you, sweetheart. Ronald.

P.S. And the Princess and Froggy lived happily ever after. (Oh, yes, he was a real Frog, all right. But the Princess was fond of him, and without her contacts could hardly tell he wasn't a Prince. Of course, since she was a real Princess, their children were all real Princes and Princesses also, except that they were green and did speak with a decided croak. But they were lovely otherwise, just like their mother.)

My father rarely wrote a letter without revealing his sense of humor. His presence surrounds me as I sort through these letters, his distinctive, slanted, half-cursive, half-printed handwriting announcing himself on the outside of each envelope: *I am here. I am still very much alive!*

The only other letter that I found of my mother's is written while she's sitting up in bed in her room on Winans Avenue, just after her flight across the Atlantic. She writes,

It's rather strange, but it's difficult for me to express my love. I feel I cannot convey the depth of my feeling and if I try it doesn't sound as sincere as I feel . . . I am overwhelmed at how this came about.

She hasn't slept in 35 hours and is tired and rambling in her letter, about her love, about the upcoming plans, and how her family wants her to stay with them longer than just one week.

She also warns him about her physical appearance. Somewhere in Europe, she rode a motorbike and fell off. She may have been on the back of the bike with a man. She doesn't recall any of the details of the accident now, but vaguely remembers it involved another man. She writes to my father:

Ronald dear, maybe I should tell you that I'm in terrible condition: I've gained weight in awkward places, I've got 4 additional scars from my accident, and my feet are completely ruined. I can't even wear high heels. I did so much walking in Europe that I have bunions, swollen feet, and even a fallen arch.

Good grief, woman.

She asks him at the end of her letter, *Ronald, is it really true?*

Marry Me Stop

Friday, 18 Jan 1963
Dearest Miriam,

<u>Now</u> you tell me. Here I am coming to you in all my handsomeness (your word), magnificent physique, the glass of fashion, the paragon of nature, etc., etc. And you? Bunions, fallen arches, weight in awkward places, four <u>more</u> scars. Really, Miriam, you'll have to do some tall cooking to make up for your deficiencies.

Despite all, he says: *I feel we should waste no time before getting married when you get here.*

My mother flew to California and they married on January 31st, 1963, in a chapel on the campus at Berkeley. My mother's younger brother, Tim, was there with his wife, and of course Elaine. At the time of my mother's wedding, Elaine already had a toddler and a baby. She writes me now that those years were a haze due to a lack of sleep and even though I have a picture of her at my mother's wedding, Elaine doesn't remember the day. This is what she remembers: they were still consulting each other about clothes. Elaine writes,

Did she ever tell you that she was married in a very slim form-fitting white dress and the sales woman told her she mustn't wear panties under it because it would show lines under the dress? I, being the prude that I was, told her she must wear underwear or it would look like she was too eager. She never told me whether she listened to my advice or the saleswoman.

"So, Mom," I ask her, "did you or didn't you?" She chuckles and says, "Let that be a mystery."

Chapter Eight

My father's first job as a newly married man was in Los Altos, about an hour down the bay from Berkeley. They lived in his little cottage near Foothill Community College located on a beautiful campus at the base of Los Altos Hills. My brother, Blake, helped me fill in the pieces of this part of their lives because this was the year that he came to live with them. They eventually moved to a larger house where Blake had his own room.

My mother says she didn't think of her newly acquired step-children as her children—they were teenagers, after all—but that they were always family. Blake describes the time he spent with Miriam and our father similarly, as family. Blake was nowhere near achieving his full potential as a student at Berkeley High. In fact, he was failing everything and in a terrible state, as he recalls. Miriam, however, willingly accepted him into their lives. He says,

Miriam worked as an assistant to the person in charge of Admissions at Los Altos High. I transferred there (I had to repeat the

second semester of my junior year) despite some reservations on the part of the Admissions Officer. Miriam told him that Daddy had said that he expected me to get straight A's. (That was the bar that Daddy set.) The Admissions Officer scoffed at the idea. We proved him wrong.

They lived like a family. Blake and my mother had some good laughs together, she always had food on the table for him when he came home from school at Los Altos High, and when President Kennedy was shot, they cried together. I asked my mother if she remembers this. She says she remembers the whole nation crying. "There were no party lines," she says. "Everyone cried."

Blake also remembers visits from my mother's brother and how he and Daddy enjoyed each other's humor. My mom made fondue for dinner one night (of course she did—it was the 1960s!) and that was the focus of their humor. "Fondue to you too," Tim and my father quipped. In an email to me, Blake says of their lives together,

Daddy worked evenings . . . I sometimes went to the college with him and studied there. I also used their Olympic-size swimming pool, which was great. Daddy ran a pretty tight ship on all fronts. At first, it worked reasonably well. Miriam made fabulous meals; I worked hard at school; Daddy worked at a job he came to hate and had a lot of tension with his supervisor (a story that repeated itself with several more jobs) . . . Every week she had a list of chores she wanted me to accomplish. If I fell short, I would be given a going over.

Go, Mom. Way to be assertive and lay down the rules!

At some point in their early years together my mother worked on her master's degree. My mother did not want to study any more, but my father was a proponent of advanced education, and she had a hard time getting out of it. My mother was practically dragged up and down the coast by my father who was determined to help her get a second degree.

I grew up hearing about how, when you're told no, to talk to the person in charge. How my mother got her M.A. is cited as the prime example of why one should do that. My father saw a notice on a bulletin board advertising an M.A. program in counseling. Only, it was the last day to enroll and anyway, the program was full. I can hear my father saying, in his confident, never-take-no-for-an-answer voice, "Let me speak to the person in charge." The person in charge said to my parents that if she wanted to enroll she'd have to have her transcripts on her desk by the next day. But her transcripts were in Berkeley! That's quite a drive up the bay, there and back in one day. But up they drove. Again, in Berkeley, they were told no. She'd have to *apply* for the transcripts; she'd have to wait. "Let me speak to the person in charge." Transcripts in hand, they drove back down the bay, had them on the right desk the following day, and my mom was enrolled in a master's program at San Jose State.

She would never have known at the time how significant that degree was to become. A decade or so later, it was her degree that saved our family. My father lost his job when I was 10 and for the rest of my childhood, my mother was the sole wage earner for our family of five.

Tensions between my mother and father were already starting to mount, even in that first year of marriage. It's not surprising that they had major differences given the gap between their ages. The one area, Blake says, that they had in common was, "their commitment to their religious faith (even though this was, as you know, separate from any form of established religion)." They said grace every night before a meal, and kept that routine throughout their lives.

The birth of Barth at the end of November 1963, Blake notes, brought "happiness, affection, and diversion." My mother likes to say, every single year on my brother's birthday, "You were the most beautiful thing I'd ever seen."

Blake must have been pretty happy with his new brother, too—a cute, little red-headed thing. The second most beautiful thing my mother had ever seen came a year and a half later. (*Hello*—Me!) As the story of my birth goes, my father had his eyes fixed straight ahead of him on the road and was so eager to get my mother to the hospital when she went into labor that he nearly missed the turn. "Ronald! There's the turn!" my mother screamed from the backseat. They made it to the hospital. I flew out, ready and eager to face the whole big, damn, wide, beautiful world. Even though my nose was apparently twisted up and they had to pinch it a bit to straighten it out. And then—*Voila!*—I was *per*fect!

Blake says of that period of time, "Setting high standards for my performance and behavior; and the whole familial set up, which very much included Miriam, was life-saving." But by the time Barth and I came around, Blake was pretty much ready to live alone. With a toddler and an infant in the house, his timing was excellent. "I applied for college and got in to St. John's (the only college Daddy really recognized)."

My father's dual passion for most of his adult life was great books and St. John's College. These passions were born by stumbling upon a great books class led by Robert Hutchens and

Mortimer Adler at the University of Chicago, well before his California days, and listening to the back and forth exchanges of ideas. This is also where he met his first wife, Eleanor. He was busing tables at the International Student Center when Eleanor asked him for a seat. Instead of taking her directly to her seat, to be funny, he took her the long way around; she evidently thought it was funny, too. He didn't get into the university where she was enrolled as a student, so he audited the class taught by Hutchens and Adler. Eleanor was also in that class.

Around the same time, a small school in Annapolis, Maryland, was struggling financially due to the Depression. The school's last-ditch effort to save itself was to hire Stringfellow Barr as president and Scott Buchannan as dean, both prominent educators. The two of them founded the New Program at St. John's College in 1937. The course of study was the great books; there were no majors or departments and all classes were discussions—of Plato, Socrates, Euclid, Newton—all the classics. Barr and Buchannan were academic revolutionaries. Previously, St. John's—founded in 1696 as King William's School—was considered a local school. Now, with the New Program, it received attention from students all over the nation.

My father was an intellectual giant, although he would claim that he was "uneducated" because he did not have what he considered a real education. He read Kierkegaard; he was profoundly influenced by Martin Buber's "I and Thou" as well as the Christian theologian, Reinhold Niebuhr, who, incidentally, married my father and Eleanor. These were academic names I'd heard in my household all through my youth, and of course all the old classics:

Marry Me Stop

Shakespeare, Thomas Hardy, Charles Dickens. My father was a voracious reader. But, according to him, a real education would only have been at St. John's—or at least a replica of the liberal arts program and discussion method—where four of his children did, in fact, receive degrees: Blake and Amiel with an undergraduate degree, and Raissa and I with a master's. Raissa was the offspring in the family who put her degree from St. John's into practice over a 37-year career as a high school great books teacher. My father was so proud of her success as a teacher. When Blake got accepted into St. John's back in 1965, my father must have been over the moon. His son was going to get the education that *he* never did.

Above and beyond the intellectual stimulation that surrounded our household and the older set of kids, we were all influenced by our half-siblings' inherent kindness. From the day we entered the world, they took a deep and lasting interest in our lives.

Talitha, at 16, couldn't wait until her little brother was born. How she absolutely adored him, and then *me*. After we were born, my parents began to make their way east, first to St. Paul, Minnesota, where Talitha also came to live with us for a short while.

Food played a central role in my parents' lives together. It may have been in St. Paul where the rice pudding recipe was found. Talitha's memory of this event is not pretty: Daddy wanted my mother to find and re-create a recipe of rice pudding that he'd had long ago. Tali remembers my mother looking long and hard for a replica that smacked of that exact taste—and presenting him with pudding after pudding—and not getting the right one. She says it was like watching a king sit on his throne, sending it all away.

But, happily, that is not how my mother remembers this now. She remembers it as wanting to please him, and when she finally found the right recipe—the secret ingredient was a whole orange peel simmered with the milk and rice, adding that unique essence— it was a eureka moment for both of them. As my father's children grew to love Miriam, they grew to love her cooking, too. If there is one member of the family who best describes the meals my mother used to make, it is Talitha. She had her first taste in St. Paul.

I was four in 1969 when we moved to Berea, Ohio, where my father was hired as a librarian in the Adult Education Department of the Cuyahoga County Public Library in Cleveland. This was a really lucky break for my father, perhaps the most prestigious job of his career. He was able to support his growing family. Berea is where my parents bought a house and finally settled, and where I grew up.

If I have it correctly, it was at that last interview where my father's confidence showed itself to be unwavering. When he was asked by his future employer if he'd feel comfortable answering some questions about the issues of the day he looked her straight on and responded by saying, "Ask me anything." There was very little that unnerved him. No one intimidated my father.

Chapter Nine

My father was not born a Landor. That was a name he gave himself when he was 16, after the English poet Walter Savage Landor. That's also when he quit school and ran away from home.

He was born a Weissfeld in Harlem, New York, in 1915. His family later moved to Washington Heights and at 16 he wanted to run from his family and thereby his Jewish identity. I've imagined the pain surrounding his leaving. I know nothing of that and heard very little about his family when I was growing up.

His father, a movie producer for a time in NYC, may have had some money. There's a large, blown-up photo of my father at his Bar Mitzvah, at age 13 in 1929. It's a grand, lavish affair. The ballroom is filled with men and women at round tables, elegant stemware and dishes, feathers in hats, all the children at one table. My father is sitting in the front row in a line of chairs smack in the middle of all his relatives. My father's mother's name was Celia, and Ronnie was her only son (his father had a son and daughter from a previous marriage) and in this photo my father is grinning from ear to ear. He is also sitting next to his maternal grandmother—my great grandmother and also my namesake. It was a happy occasion, and they must have been so proud of him. A few years later, he was gone—out of their lives completely.

My father must have known when he chose his new name that he was using an anagram—Landor and Ronald have the same letters. At an early age he was clever, and developed an appreciation for poetry. But it remains a mystery why he was so intent on separating himself from his true identity.

By making this choice, he rejected his mother, his father, his siblings, and possibly friends in order to go after an idea, proving early on that philosophy—ideas—were more important to him than his closest relations. Although, I think this was largely a front, a disguise of some deeper pain that he never discussed with me, and that I never really understood. My father was a deeply feeling man. Only a deeply feeling man could be so moved as he was—even as an adult—by the Broadway musicals of the 1940s. He loved those old musicals and we grew up on them, listening to the records after dinner and learning all the songs. He would get teary by the power of the love expressed in some of the old classics, *Carrousel, Fiddler on the Roof.* I think of my own relations with my father and the riches it held.

My dad had a great, comfy lap for a little girl to sit on. He'd smoke his cigar and afterwards his clothes smelled of a comfort that I nuzzled into. When he leaned with his back against the living room heater on a snowy day, I put my arms around him and my head just reached up to his slightly plump belly, and I rested my head there with Daddy's arms around me. He taught me how butterflies kiss, blinking his eyelashes on my cheek and how Eskimos kiss, rubbing noses. He read me stories—"Little Black Sambo," "Where the Wild Things Are," "Peter Rabbit,"—and said prayers with Barth and me, kneeling in front of my bed before going to sleep.

My father chose my name after his grandmother, whom he loved. But it was the German pronunciation, with a hard g, and everyone kept saying it wrong! At an early age, this bugged me. A simpler name would have suited me. I heard a name that sounded much prettier and when we were at a concert given by a folk musician who strummed a guitar, I eagerly raised my hand when he asked for some children in the audience to come up on stage. He spotted the five-year-old redhead in the crowd and called on me.

My parents' eyes would shine, the way they describe that moment—of their little girl up there, standing at the end of a line of other children on the edge of the stage, primping herself, pulling up her socks, smoothing back her hair, and waiting her turn for a song to be sung about *her*. My parents say that I was so adorable the audience thought I was planted up there. I didn't know I was being cute. All I was doing was getting ready for my big moment. Then it came. All the other kids had had their turn and I was left alone on stage with the singer. When he asked me what my name was, I felt that I had only one choice. I said loudly and boldly into the microphone, "JANE!"

It's one of my earliest memories—being up on the stage and then walking out of the auditorium and into the sunlight, my mother pushing a stroller and both of my parents still laughing—saying to some of the other audience members, "That's not really her name!"

My father delighted in me—I was his little girl—and I know that he admired the woman I grew up to be.

As to his opinions, however, he clung to them with an iron fist. He would not let them go, however wrong he was proven to be, however many people there were in the room attempting to get him to change his mind. No. He was fierce.

My mother tried so hard to please him. I cringe now when I think of the demands he made on her, even when she was pregnant. He didn't like for her to lie down when she was tired, like he had some image in his mind of how a strong woman should be in her pregnancy, and it wasn't lying down. I think of my own pregnancy—and how appalling this is and how unknowing he was. I was exhausted all of the time. My mother needed to get up from the couch when he came home—not wanting him to know she was resting. Like she was some character in the book "The Good Earth"—going back to the field to work after cutting her own child's umbilical cord. My dad admired that kind of stalwart homemaker and had an idealized, unrealistic notion of what it meant to be a woman.

If there's a story that shows how stubborn my father was, it is best illustrated in my memory of our family discussion of the movie "Shirley Valentine," a 1989 British romantic comedy.

Our argument was about the main character in the movie, Shirley, and how my father thought she was wrong to have left her husband, however miserable she was. Never mind that it wouldn't have been a movie if the director just let poor Shirley suffer with her controlling ogre of a husband. She hightailed it to Greece and had a love affair. My father argued and stuck to his guns about how wrong this was. Never *mind* how she was treated by her insufferable husband and how, in the end, the affair actually proves to be beneficial to both of them. The affair, and taking time away from her husband, allows her to reclaim herself and to feel like a woman again. Her husband sees her in Greece sitting quietly at a table on the edge of the sea drinking a glass of wine, and he walks right past her, not recognizing her. She's a changed woman. He realizes how he's taken her for granted, and we are left to believe that they will reunite. Shirley felt beautiful again, and to the husband's credit, he allows himself to soften at her renewed femininity. For my father this movie smacked of "women's lib," a term he hated. My father deplored this movie.

We argued long and hard to try to get him to see it otherwise. To see it for the beautiful, hard lessons learned. I don't think the director's point was to show that a bad marriage is fixable by simply having an affair. The point was that something extreme had to be done in order for Shirley to feel whole again—even if it meant breaking vows. Sometimes there are exceptions to the rules. And Shirley needed to regain her sense of self. My father was not to be swayed. Not on Shirley Valentine, not on anything.

He was "of another generation," an excuse my mother gave for him time after time—when he'd pronounce that "children should be seen but not heard," or when he'd make statements like, "a woman's place is in the home."

Those proclamations had nothing to do with his generation. Not everybody in his generation thought this way and it's not his generation's fault that he was close-minded and limited in his thinking around these issues. My Uncle Victor insightfully notes in his correspondence to me that the psychological bonding my mother had with her father led to the kind of man she married. It's never escaped me how protective she has always been of her father and her husband. Both men who were much older than their wives, who held firm, old-fashioned convictions, and who were ultimately unfulfilled in their work life.

The thing that's always puzzled me about my father's determined way of arguing was that I never, ever witnessed him being swayed by anyone else's opinion. I never remember him ever saying, I see what you mean, or, I never saw it that way before. Which is ironic, given his love of the St. John's method of education, of learning through discussing, and of listening to other points of view.

My father had a Biblical quote hanging on his study wall: "Come let us reason together." The everlasting irony is that my father believed in this philosophy in the core of his being— he breathed it—but he didn't practice it where it mattered the most—in his own home. When he had an opinion, he wouldn't change it. It wouldn't really matter what argument I, or my mother, put forth. How we wished it had mattered. If there is one thing I have learned from my parents' marriage, it's how important it is to compromise. They did not compromise. My mother lives with regrets because she was unwilling to come to his terms. And he was unwilling to come to hers. They fought bitterly.

As to the possibility of my parents ever seeking marital counseling, we could forget about it. My father mocked the entire field of psychological analysis.

It's pretty much common knowledge that things that are too painful to look at are buried, so that even I forgot some of the memories of how Daddy used to scorn the practice of therapy. "Don't you remember how Daddy used to say 'feelings schmeelings'?" Amiel asked me. And then I did remember. It all came rushing back and I remembered the shame I felt around that, that my father who was so wise and witty and smart would think that seeking counseling was a weakness rather than a strength. The one time my mother managed to get him into a therapist's office, she said he sat in stony silence. He bitterly ridiculed the whole idea of it.

He was a deeply private man. But he was also undoubtedly terrified of waking up a sleeping dragon of emotions that had been buried for decades. That dragon would remain dormant and he would go to his grave without ever talking about his pain with another person, such as a professional counselor. It's my uneducated guess that he would have been a far less angry man if he had been willing to unleash some of that pain, especially in regard to his own mother, and whatever happened in his childhood, and why he left his family.

My father had some weapons in his arsenal that he used throughout my childhood that were hurtful to our family. He would retreat. Once, when I was about ten, he moved out altogether. He moved into an apartment for a while in Berea. He moved to Chicago to live with my sister, on and off. For a time in the early '70s, when my mother was alone with three children and my sister not yet five, he moved to Israel. He sent home beautifully detailed letters of his time there and my mother dutifully typed them all and put them in a binder for keepsake. I don't know how my mother accepted this situation. Maybe she simply did not have a say in the matter regarding his leaving. He went to Israel a second time, thinking he would reunite himself with his true, Jewish identity—he had thoughts of finding work there and perhaps moving there for good. Not surprisingly, this attempt was not a success and he came home. And my mother supported him throughout this self-search, financially and spiritually.

His greatest weapon, which he wielded throughout my childhood, was his silence. When he and my mother fought—usually over something trivial, anything could tip the mood—he would go up into his study in the attic and not come down for dinner. This could last for days or weeks at a time. He would ignore her and us altogether. The roar of his silence was deafening, reverberating throughout the house and spilling over into most aspects of my life. I had trouble in school and with friends. My father, who ironically was writing a book on education, didn't want to deal with it. Or he didn't know how to deal with it. He wouldn't speak to me when I came home from school with natty hair and some girl's blood in my fingernails, and talk to me about what was going on. This was not the image he wanted of his little girl.

It was most awful when he spoke to my mother in a demeaning way, or when he refused to speak to her altogether. He would lock himself away and the pain of their contention was all over my mother's face, an open wound we could do nothing to salve.

Marry Me Stop

All joy was extinguished and would not resurface until the moods passed, but who knew when that would be? Blake said to me once that so much of their fighting when we were kids had to do with the right way to raise us. But as far as he could see, we were thriving! What were they fighting about? Maybe it was my father's urge to get it all right the second time around. He had a formula and he didn't want to relinquish that. If there were too many steps around that formula, there was a fight.

I realize now that anger is a choice. My father could have made more choices not to be angry—like he always did on Christmas when he was never angry and he rose to the occasion and it was a happy time—and I wish that he had. The light of the holiday season was so often extinguished once the evergreen was tossed out.

However, despite his contentious behavior and unrelenting, strict philosophies of right and wrong, my father loved us. He loved us all more than anything in the world and he repeated this refrain throughout our lives. My father loved research and he loved his children, and he tirelessly combined those two passions to find the very best for us that life had to offer and still remain within our somewhat meager financial range.

For me, that included summer camp, a nanny position with family friends in London and then theatre school there, an agricultural farm and university program in Israel, cooking school in New York City, the University of St. Andrews in Scotland, St. John's College, and finally a teaching internship program at the University of New Mexico, which led me to a ten-year teaching career. My father researched and found every single one of those situations for me. He and my mother even found one of my best living situations. They were back at a public library scanning that beloved bulletin board again—in Santa Fe—discussing my living prospects when a woman overheard them speaking. *She* had a room and *yes* it was available. That woman became a great moral influence in my life. I lived with Cathie for two years, as did my sister, Amiel, while she attended St. John's, at their Santa Fe campus. I lived in a beautiful, sun-filled room that looked out onto the hills in a house that Cathie built by herself with her own two hands.

We had a motto in our family: "T.D." Trust Daddy. This motto did not work for all of my siblings. I know that. But it worked for me. I did trust Daddy. He helped give shape and structure to my life. Whenever I was floundering and looking around, wondering, What next? What now? Daddy would come up with a plan. We were a great team. He did the research and I always followed through. When I was accepted into the teaching internship program, at a time in my life when I really didn't know what I was going to do, I called him on the phone and told him the good news. He was so relieved for me I could hear him holding back his tears.

Wherever I lived, I wrote letters home. My parents and I kept up a regular correspondence with each other always. One letter from my father in particular stands out. I had failed my end-of-the-year written exams at the University of London. I was 19 and, rightly so, the university committee said I needed to wait a few years before I was ready again to tackle the rigors of university, especially a British one. I wrote my parents to tell them how ashamed I was.

Marry Me Stop

My father could not have written a more compassionate reply. The theme of his letter was how everyone has known failure. The best actors and the best athletes. You cannot succeed without knowing what it means to fail, he wrote. These were the most encouraging words he could have said and they have comforted me all of my life. When I was left in London wondering, What next, I mentioned Israel to my dad and he got right on it. He found a six-month kibbutz and university program for me. My parents flew to London, and then saw me board a plane for my next big adventure.

My father taught me about writing and he taught me to use the dictionary because words mattered. He loved words and told me there was hardly a day that went by where he didn't consult his dictionary. But there was one word, he told me once, that he didn't like. That word was "fun." It was a typical, dour announcement. The word was too trivial, it was empty, and it lacked meaning. There's another irony, because my dad had such a *sense* of fun. In some of his rare moods, he delighted us with his sense of fun. He once scoured the neighborhood looking for his three children and then took us on a spontaneous trip to an amusement park two hours away. My father was behind another memorable, adventurous scheme. Late one night, our parents came into our bedroom to wake us. They told us to get dressed and we all piled into the car. Where are we *going*, we all wondered. My father was in high spirits. "Let's follow that car," he said. The car in front of us had a bumper sticker that said "Barnhills." We followed the car and ended up at the grand opening of a large, candy-filled ice cream parlor in the center of the Berea Commons. We all delightfully enjoyed an ice cream cone—at midnight.

My five siblings and I may have disagreements about Daddy and what kind of man he was. Each of us had our own relationship with him. But one area we all agreed on was his sense of humor. No one doubted it and everyone appreciated it. He kept a life-long, humorous correspondence with his old pal from New York, Ivan. The missives the two of them sent back and forth to each other over the years were the work of artists, cleverly crafted letters keeping each man on his toes. And throughout our lives, he made every one of us laugh.

Someone once captured our delight in Daddy's humor, snapped in a single moment, a photo of my siblings and I crowded around him on a couch. We are all laughing hard, caught right at the apex of the moment. Tali and I have our heads thrown back. My father is laughing himself at his own witty joke. We are all in fits over whatever hilarious and amusing thing he had just said.

The week—every year—between Christmas and New Year's when Raissa, Blake, and Talitha, and then Lyn, Blake's wife, came to Berea are some of the happiest memories I have of my childhood. No matter what was happening between my mother and father, no matter what disagreements they were arguing over now, Daddy would snap out of it and be cheerful. Food made my father very happy, and there was always a lot going on in the kitchen the week before. We were preparing for my siblings' arrival and as I grew older, I was steeped in the cooking and preparing process with my mom.

Marry Me Stop

If my mom didn't brag about her own cooking abilities, my older siblings sung her praises for her. Talitha reminisces about the meals as if she is describing a culinary adventure like none other. We all remember the baked crab on toast, the Canadian cheese soup, and the soup soubise, a curried soup with onions. We made fresh, out-of-the-oven popovers, a savory muffin with an eggy dough. Tali remembers the beef Wellington, beef wrapped in puff pastry and baked. My mother never forgot the chopped chicken liver my father prepared for her in the early days, and she later found a recipe with lots of butter, lots of sautéed onions, and sherry. We ate that spread on a fresh bagel in the afternoons with a cup of tea. And it would not have been a holiday without blintzes—stacks of them which my mother made well in advance and put in the freezer—or a Lindy's cheesecake, with grated lemon rind and about eight packages of cream cheese. Or we made coffee cream cake, a thinly serrated white cake soaked in coffee syrup and layered with whipped cream. Tubs of spritz butter cookies were usually on hand. Many of these recipes—the blintzes, chopped liver, cheesecake—were the food my father remembers from growing up in New York. These meals were a labor of love. Once, when I was helping my mother clean out some papers while home from college, I found pages and pages of neatly typed menus from those Christmas holidays.

Sure, during the holidays disagreements arose and arguments between my father and one of my older siblings could last for days. Long discussions took place between them; usually about books I hadn't yet read or about something I didn't understand, such as why *couldn't* my brother and his girlfriend sleep in the same room? (I understood it, but I didn't *get* it.) But mostly the house was enlivened by humor and good cheer. I remember hearing my father and one of my older siblings hooting with laughter over a cartoon from "The New Yorker." Or maybe he was laughing with Barbara Parry, his old friend from Berkeley whom Raissa lived with in Amherst when she was 18 and who spent many holidays with us. Perhaps Barbara brought the cartoon. It was of two characters—maybe pigs?—one saying to the other, "I'm more erudite than you." I didn't even know what that meant (so I knew I had a lot of catching up to do in the erudition department.)

We played charades on New Year's Eve—Barbara was an expert, keeping us in line with the rules—and we took long walks in the metro parks in the snow. When I was still young enough, Blake delighted me by putting me on his shoulders for a stroll around the block. He was six foot three and there I was, on top of the world! No other kids in the neighborhood had siblings who would appear in the winter, and in the summers, too, and provide merriment and diversion in the way that they did. My father helped keep the warm bonds strong between us and my mother stoked the warmth with her cooking, her generosity, her love and good humor, and her acceptance of them.

Chapter Ten

When my sister Amiel was five years old, I was ten, and my brother Barth was 12, my mother started looking for work. Thankfully, she had that degree because my father was let go from his job. He'd written a letter of complaint about his supervisor, which his colleagues agreed to sign with him. In the end they backed out—afraid of losing their own jobs—and my father was left signing it alone. The supervisor fired him; subsequently, the supervisor was fired, proving the validity of my father's dispute. The lawyer whom my father hired to go to court over this injustice neglected to file the paperwork on time—another irony given my father's meticulousness and punctuality on all things—and it became a lost cause. My mother was forced to save the family.

She became a junior high school counselor and she loved her work. Helping kids in school, talking to parents, guiding kids in the right direction with their course work—it was what she loved and she was an expert and loved by those kids. My father was a wonderful listener, and she'd often bring her work issues home with her, talking about her day at the dinner table, about colleagues, principals, students, and teachers. My mom was particularly sensitive to the kids' needs and thought it inexcusable when she heard teachers speaking disparagingly about students.

A kid whom I remember her talking about had a lot of trouble in school—maybe he was failing—and he got into a fight with another kid. There was something he excelled in, however, and that was art. As a form of punishment, the principal decided that he should get pulled from art, because he loved it so much. That'll show him. The art teacher deplored this decision and so did my mother. No matter how terrible a kid he is, you don't take away the one thing in which he is excelling. It's that one thing that's going to *keep* his head above water and *help* turn him around. I don't know whatever happened, but I know my mother fought for him.

Maybe it was hearing stories like this that prompted my sister, Amiel, to also become someone who fights for the underdog. She was five years younger than me, and a little spitfire rebel. If there ever was a little maverick like none other running around the neighborhood, it was she. When she grew up a bit and decided, Yeah, I guess I'll start wearing a top at the public swimming pool, it became her mission on the way to and from school to stand up for the kids who were being picked on. No one was going to bully her and no one was going to bully the little black boys from the Children's Home. She defended them. She even brought a little overweight boy who had no friends home from school one day, probably to give him some cookies. My mom set up that example for her.

Marry Me Stop

Amiel stood by those kids and came to their aid. She laughs as she recalls one little black boy she used to walk with and says, "His name was Johnny Walker." At an early age, she was aware of people's wounds and vulnerability, so that even now, as an adult, Amiel has chosen a profession—counseling—to help people advance themselves. She recently had a success story of helping a struggling high school student get accepted into engineering school —after he had decided to just go work in a factory. She was the first person he texted when he got the acceptance letter and on his birthday he made sure to save Amiel a piece of his cake. "People will shoot low out of fear," she says. She helped save this kid from doing menial work and helped him see his higher potential.

How like my mother! This was my mother's battle cry: help get young kids into college. Whenever she had the opportunity, she would talk to a young person about the advantages of a higher education. She'd say to them, Look, even if you drop out of school you can still go to community college! She'd work long and hard at helping a kid advance his or her lot. She never forgot when that 16-year-old girl ran up to her when she was visiting a community college and said, "Mrs. Landor! I wouldn't be here if it weren't for you!" She helped people set a goal and reach it because she believed that everyone has potential. She believed she did, too. It's how she was able to graduate from high school, leave her small town, go abroad and see a bit of the world, and get a degree that would help her family survive. She understood the power of a college degree.

My mother did not just support her family or the troubled kids she saw every day at school; when she saw a need, she reached out. I had a friend in high school that was miserably picked on—she was smarter than all those nasty teenagers—and she came from a difficult home. We worked together at the local movie theatre. My mother knew of this girl, but not very well—she'd only heard stories about her hard times. It was Christmas and my mother walked up to the outside booth where my friend was selling the movie tickets, and gave her a wrapped present. It was a jewelry box, with a twenty-dollar bill inside.

She believed in herself, she believed in others, and she believed in me. Her support was immediate and she was always available. When I was in elementary school getting into fights with kids at school, she'd help untangle my hair, soothe me, talk to me. Once, at one of those unfortunate sleepovers that is a rite-of-passage for some teens, I became the center of bullying and spent the night with my head in my sleeping bag—the horrible beasties on the outside teasing me relentlessly. In the early morning hours, I called my mom and she came over right away to get me.

When I was older and home from college, it was winter and terrible weather and Amiel and I borrowed the car and as I was driving through an intersection, another driver rammed into us. I called my mom from a gas station, sobbing. I could hear the panic in her voice when she asked about Amiel. When I told her she was fine, my mom just kept saying over and over again that the car doesn't matter.

My mother's face is an open book. There's no mystery there. Her pain is there; her love is there. A very brief, fleeting moment occurred once that she was unaware of, but that has always stayed with me. We were driving in the opposite direction. I saw her in the other lane across from me, in her own car, but she didn't see me. She was looking straight ahead, watching the road. I was so happy to see her and I was watching her face, watching her open expression, on the cusp of a full-blown smile, if only I could catch her eye. I waited for it, that burst of affirmation that I knew would appear on her face, a gush of light and love. I was waving at her, trying to get her attention. Then I remembered the horn! But it was too late. She drove right on by and I felt like it was a missed moment, that excitement we would have shared together at serendipitously seeing each other on the road.

My mom was busy at work and supporting our family, but she wasn't above thinking about fashion. I don't think my father argued with her about her buying clothes because maybe he knew he'd better not. She was the one bringing home the salary. She discovered TJ Maxx and loved coming home from work with her bundles and proclaiming how much money she saved. Never mind how much I've spent—look how much I've saved! My father was amused by her proclamation, and thankfully I think he let it go.

With her lost shoe from her childhood, her outgrown cape, and the guilt from her teenage years of owning a necklace she didn't feel was rightfully hers, Miriam developed a resolve as a young adult to turn her fortune around. Clothes became important to her. I see this in every old black and white photo of her. And there are a lot! As a young adult, boy did she love to pose in front of the camera. There she is, in yet *another* bathing suit.

In a wintry-looking photo taken in a park years later my mother is holding my brother, who was two. She is smiling, happy to be with whomever took the photo, the wind blowing her skirt to one side. She dressed nothing like I dressed when I had a two-year-old on my hip. I lived in tee shirts and jeans for about six years after my babies were born. In this photo in the park, my mom is wearing a wide, '50s style pink skirt, a tight, white sweater with three-quarter length sleeves, and a white, wool tam o' shanter—a Scottish cap with a pom-pom—on the side of her head. She looks so natural and comfortable in her get-up; she could be posing for L.L. Bean.

In all the photos that were taken of my mother when I was growing up, she looks fabulous. She dressed up on Christmas day especially. Flowing, floral dresses; slim-fitting dresses that accentuated her figure; green, silky, low-cut dresses. At an outdoor wedding we went to when I was about twelve, we're posing with the family of the groom, my mother unquestionably more stylish than the mother of the groom: she's wearing pale yellow—a slim-fitting skirt with a very thin yellow belt and a smart-looking, very fashionable, silky yellow blouse with a subtle print of a giraffe running down one side of it.

I knew early on that my mom loved clothes, watching her dress for a party, or for work. She was probably the best-dressed staff member in the entire school. Other women told her so. She was slim, she was blond, she was tall, she was friendly, she was warm. She was well accessorized, too: handbags, belts, pendants, necklaces, scarves, and hats, which she wore with style over her short, wavy blond hair. Women she worked with didn't begrudge her good taste, probably because there wasn't an ounce of vanity about her. Her bright, blue eyes and her broad, wide face with Lithuanian and German features, wore a friendly, open expression. She let people in and she comforted them with her ability to listen.

Marry Me Stop

My father secluded himself in his study and wrote volumes of poetry, all those years in Berea. I'd come home from high school and whip up a batch of cookies and bring them up to him on a plate with a glass of milk. I'd sit on the attic steps and we'd talk. Maybe his idea of cooking school for me started brewing while enjoying those plates of cookies.

My parents continued to fight about child-rearing all throughout my growing up, but somewhere along the winding, tumultuous path of their marriage, their love for each other blossomed anew. They decided to hold a rededication ceremony in a church we occasionally attended. My father wrote a poem for my mother, an asking-for-forgiveness of sorts, during that period of renewed love.

A Secret Way, for Miriam

How could I ever hope to tell it all?
of how I reaped where I had never sowed—
given a gift of love instead of gall?

I hid from truth that I deserved to fall,
Yet it was only love that Love bestowed.
How could I ever hope to tell it all?

Suffering proved the key to the sacred scrawl,
which broke for me the secret of the code:
given a gift of love instead of gall!

Regina Landor

I know nothing—I have no wherewithal—
Except where love has taken up abode.
How could I ever hope to tell it all?

What once I thought as triumphs—now appall.
But tears can win and grace in us explode,
given a gift of love instead of gall.

In time that's left before the final call,
before I come to running out of road,
how could I ever hope to tell it all—
given a gift of love instead of gall?

Chapter Eleven

Although my mother was a good decision-maker on the home front, she was on the fence when it came to politics and religion. Always a Democrat, she was never a die-hard liberal. She boycotted table grapes in the late 1960s in support of labor unions for farm workers, but if caught in a discussion with a conservative, she would lend a sympathetic ear. My father also tended to vote as a Democrat, but he was conservative on social issues, such as abortion. Politics was an area of constant bickering between them. On religion, my mother was a Christian, but later in life, especially after my father died, she would tell people she is Jewish, probably as an attempt to sympathize with the Jewish plight and also to somehow feel closer to my father, who actually was Jewish.

In the early stages of our marriage, Billy always took the bait when she announced to people that she is Jewish. He was annoyed by it, but also managed to find a way to tease her about her claim. "Miriam," he'd say. "Is Jesus Christ your savior?"

"Well, yes he is."

"Then you're not Jewish." End of discussion.

Where my mother's contradictions offered her perhaps the most disservice in her personal life, aside from her relationship with my father, occurred between her and one friend in particular, and that friend was Louise.

Louise was a staple of constancy and friendship, warmth and good humor during many of my early years, after I turned five when we moved to Berea. A mutual friend of my mom's and Louise's brought them together. That was Charlene, who later moved to Michigan. Traditions were built around this friendship with Louise. Annual holiday celebrations were shared together. Recipes were swapped and kept forever, secrets exchanged. Conversations on the phone, my mom in our kitchen and Louise on the other end in her kitchen could last for hours.

Louise was from the south and she had a way about her that bespoke southern gentility. She was tall with brown hair cut in a bob that swayed when she walked. Even her body swayed, like a slow moving haze of smoke, slowly curling around, wafting a hint of her alluring and mysterious scent. She had that mystique about her. Her movements were unhurried. Her speech was a drawl. Her laugh was a drawn-out chuckle. She was attractive and sassy and witty. She had an intellectual humor and subtly flirted with my father. I remember that.

She made a cake that became my brother's favorite. I still have the recipe: Louise's Chocolate Pound Cake, and I stood in her kitchen next to her at the counter watching her make it and she gave me the beaters to lick afterwards. Much later, when I had to get glasses when I was in high school, Louise came with me to try them on. And it was then that we shared our first, and perhaps only, adult exchange. I put on a pair of plastic tortoise shell glasses and turned away from the mirror and asked her what she thought. She gave me her steady, crooked smile and cupped her hand around her mouth and said in a mock whisper, "I think they make you look sexy." Sold.

For years she and my mother shared laughter and heartache. She is the friend my mother went to when the fighting between my parents reached a boiling point, when my mother needed a release, a person to hear her.

When my parents had their re-dedication ceremony, Louise did not want my mother to go through with it, my mother told me privately. This hurt her, but I think Louise was done listening to my mother cry on the phone. She urged my mother to leave my father, but she supported her all the same. She came to the ceremony and held a little party for them—and us—at her home afterwards. One year later, their continued fighting put a mockery to their dedication. Theirs was a marriage of passion and anger, disappointment and ironically, enduring love.

When Louise's own marriage fell to pieces, my impression was that my mother was not, in turn, there for her. At least that is partly my understanding of how their friendship came crashing to an end. Louise's husband was to remarry and my mother, ever faithful to that fence she perched herself on, befriended the husband's new wife. In fact, she and my father invited them over, welcomed them socially, and celebrated their marriage.

I do not know the amount of time that lapsed between the conclusion of my mother's and Louise's relationship and when my mother's friendship with Louise's ex-husband and his new wife began, but it couldn't have been too great. I suspect something else must have been the catalyst that ended her relationship with Louise. When I ask my mother now, in her declining state, if she knows why it ended she says she doesn't know. She pauses when I mention Louise, like she's still searching for an answer. "She dropped me," she says. "She received an inheritance and I suggested how she should invest it. She didn't like me interfering." I can well imagine that. My mom struggles with boundaries. But surely, there was something else. Maybe something in Louise's character that compelled her to walk away, a flaw that some souls possess that forces them to turn their backs rather than face a problem, and forgive.

My mother was kind to the new wife and befriended her. Louise was right to be hurt, if in fact that is how it really played out. It's possible my mother was reacting to being abandoned by Louise first. I don't really know what happened, only that the friendship was utterly over for good. She no longer called my mother. My mother lost her friend completely. We were no longer guests at Louise's annual Christmas party. That I do know. My father and I happened to drop by at the wrong moment, to deliver a Christmas gift—maybe a box of chocolates or a bottle of wine—and her whole table was elegantly set for a party. My father was cordial to her, but embarrassed. We exchanged niceties. She hugged me and was kind. Then we quickly left. I remember asking my father what the matter was as we returned to the car. Maybe because it had been a few years, I didn't connect the dots.

"Regina," he said, "we used to be invited to that party." That was the last time I saw Louise.

When you're a teenager, you're really only caught up in your own world, not the world of the adults around you. So to a certain extent I was oblivious to what really happened. When I got closer to my twenties, I was shocked by the absence of Louise. I was shocked by the sadness of what my mother had lost. When I'd ask her about Louise, what had happened, she'd say she didn't know. I felt she simply could not acknowledge any role that she had played in the dissolution of that friendship. No one replaced that closeness, during that period of time, that she shared as an adult with another adult friend, someone with whom she shared woes of childrearing, a new pregnancy, a troubled marriage. They were both in the same stages in life, both with children, both in difficult marriages. They leaned on each other and they must have needed each other; my mother with fewer social connections was probably the more wanting of the two.

When I came home from college in my early twenties, I felt such a loss for my mother whenever I thought of Louise.

And then a peculiar twist took place during that summer home from college. Louise kicked her daughter out of the house. Again, that was my understanding without any substantial information as to why or what happened, only that they fought and her daughter needed a place to stay. She called my parents and they took her in.

I was working at my summer restaurant job one afternoon during the time Louise's daughter was living with us when apparently Louise walked into our house, went upstairs, took her daughter's clothes out of the closet, put them into a suitcase, and left. (These were the days when front doors were never locked.) She may have interpreted my parents' willingness to help as interfering with her own most intimate relationships.

I was incredulous that my boyfriend, who was visiting, got a glimpse of Louise and I did not. "Wait, you *saw* her?"

"Yes. She came in and packed up some clothes. She asked me where I'm from." (He was German.) "She seemed very nice."

I couldn't believe I'd missed the chance of seeing her. Louise vanished from our lives so rapidly; she carried with her a mystique, and maybe even knowledge of the psychology of my own family that I yearned to possess myself. She had some of my mother's secrets. Louise was knowing and wise and also tragic, a twentieth century Scarlet O'Hara. My mother's loneliness during that period of time was undoubtedly enhanced by that unfortunate loss. She never saw Louise again.

If only she and *Elaine* could have continued growing up together, raising children, sharing their life! Sadly, the gulf between California and Ohio did not offer the opportunity for the day-to-day exchanges for which any young mother hungers. Elaine lived in our lives, but only really in stories that my mother told of their days together. Elaine's name was mentioned so often in my growing up, she could have been a neighbor down the street, or someone my mother just spent the afternoon with, so fresh were the memories that she had with her and so alive did they remain.

Marry Me Stop

The harsh turn of events, which my mother's relationship with Louise took, must have made the absence of her friendship with Elaine feel more pronounced than ever during those years.

Chapter Twelve

When my brother, sister and I moved out of the house, suddenly all these empty rooms were available! My parents used this opportunity well. They decided to rent rooms to foreign students, kids who were studying abroad at Baldwin Wallace. It was a great set-up and it worked beautifully for a time. My parents became very fond of many of the students, particularly some of the Japanese women. The families sent elaborate gifts from Japan; parents whose children were living with my parents wrote letters of gratitude and implored my parents to come visit them abroad. My mother formed a close bond with a young woman from Panama, and her siblings, too. Much later, a young man from Turkey lived in the basement apartment for a few years and he and my mother became so close, he asked her to be his surrogate mother at his wedding.

My father tired of this, however. They had several years of comings and goings of students, and he wanted his own space returned to him and solitude restored. They fought over this. The income was helping pay for college loans. My mom would not budge, and so my father moved out.

It's possible the issue of the renters is not why he left again. There were obviously bigger problems. But whatever they were, my father was once again in Chicago, in an apartment by the lake.

My mother visited him often. And maybe it was better that way. They still laughed together. They still enjoyed each other's company, sharing meals together, reading the Bible together. They never stopped loving each other.

Around this time, I was beginning my career as an elementary teacher. I loved those little kids and was told by my supervisors in my internship program in New Mexico that I was a natural. I remember thinking that each kid is like a separate file—they are each their own unique person—and I respected them and their thoughts and opinions deeply. I felt so lucky that it was kids I was working with, and *not* files, or sitting at a desk pushing paper. I got my first job as a first grade teacher in Highwood, a suburb north of Chicago.

On the very first day of school, a little boy named Danny walked into the classroom. He sat down at his desk, slumped in his chair, put his chin in his hand and shook his head sadly and said, "I'm gonna hate college."

My dad laughed so hard when I told him that story. This little kid already had a sense of what was in store for him. My dad loved hearing stories about my day in the classroom when I visited him in his apartment off Sheridan Road.

But then I started having troubles of my own in my career. That school year ended and many of the new teachers were laid off, including me. However, my principal recommended me to another school in a neighboring district, and I was hired.

Enter: another principal making unjust decisions. Like me, this principal was also new to the district. With her newly acquired power, she appeared downright eager to sink her talons into young blood that appeared on the scene, to the detriment of the new teachers wanting to make a difference in the classroom and improve the old-school ways of doing things. Threatened by me and another new teacher, her evaluations determined that we were not to be rehired.

I went to war. Every parent whose child I had in my classroom appreciated the strides I'd made with the students, in reading and writing. I individualized each student's reading program (unlike the other first grade teachers in the building who gave their students the exact same, repetitive homework, night after night, year after year) and to the embarrassment of those teachers, the PTA honored all the kids in my classroom for having "published" a book. The teachers in the other classrooms aimed low and ignored their students' potential. So, no published, student books. Very little writing, if at all, went on in their classrooms. Any writing that happened was copied from the blackboard. The wave of the district was leaning toward individualized learning; and yet, I was being criticized by my principal for doing just that. The parents in my classroom bonded together to help me save my job. They all wrote letters in support of me, and it was working.

I also wrote a defense statement. I remember my brother, Barth, saying that I write better than the principal, whose written critique of me was nonsensical. Before I turned in my statement,

I read it to my father. Some changes needed to be made, I could see that. As I read it out loud, there were some negative comments I'd made—a hint of sarcasm here and there. I'd look up at my father, who was listening attentively from the couch, and I'd say, That should go, right? And he'd nod.

My father stuck around to see me win that last battle. My job was saved. The superintendent put me in another school. "There is justice in the world after all," my father said to me. Like his own story of his supervisor who was then fired, this principal who tried to fire me also lost her job, and I was vindicated.

The doctor who diagnosed my father with an aneurysm called all the family together. We gravely stood by my father who was told that he'd maybe have a year to live before the aneurysm fatally tore his aorta. It was inoperable. That year, my siblings, who were living in the Chicago area, and I brought meals to him at his apartment every night. I drove down from Highland Park. I always made enough at dinnertime for Daddy. Once, when I brought him a plate of fish, potatoes, and probably a side of greens, which he didn't particularly like, I sat next to him at the table in his apartment as he eagerly ate the meal, enjoying every bite. He had called me earlier in the day—but I was unable to take the call. When I asked him why he'd called he said, "To tell you I wasn't hungry." We both got a kick out of that.

The night my father died, Raissa was hosting a birthday party for her daughter, for Amiel, and for me—we were all born in early May. My mom was on her way over to the party—she happened to be in Chicago at the time, staying with Barth—and my father called her and asked her to bring over a bottle of ginger ale. His stomach was not doing well.

He was actually in a lot of pain. My mother sat with him, giving up all thoughts of going to a party. They talked quietly. She gave him some of the morphine pills. He told her she was the right one to be there with him. She held his hand as she read him the 23rd Psalm. He said the words, I am not afraid, only near to death. She leaned close to his ear and told him, I am your wife. And then sometime after midnight, he took his last breath. He was 78 years old; my mom was 60.

I've always thought my dad was a gentleman for waiting until the party was over before he died.

Perhaps the very last good decision my mother made before her life took an unfortunate turn can be added to her checklist of good decisions she's made in her life. Just days after retiring from her 20-year career when she was 62, she started to get headaches. She decided to take them seriously and went in to see her doctor. The MRI revealed a brain aneurysm and she had to make a decision: continue living a healthy life but risk the aneurysm bursting, or have surgery. A hole was drilled through her skull and a metal clip was put on the aneurysm. The surgery may have saved her life. But it also changed the course of her life. She could no longer drive safely, for one. The seizures that followed put into motion the downward spiral of memory loss and over time, dementia.

Miriam and her sister, Ruth, circa 1940

Miriam in her precious cape

Regina Landor

Mim with her brother, Jimmy

Jimmy made everyone laugh.

Marry Me Stop

Mim and her sister, Ann

The fastest typist in town

Regina Landor

High School Graduation, 1952

Party time!

Bathing Beauty

Mim with brothers Victor and David

Regina Landor

Mim and Vic

Elaine and Mim

Marry Me Stop

Traveling with Elaine

Mile-long legs

Wedding Day, January 31, 1963

Miriam with her first-born, Barth

Ronald with Miriam and baby Barth

Blake-Barth-Ronald   Dec. 1963

Daddy with his two sons

Miriam holding Barth, with Raissa and Blake, pregnant with me

Miriam with Barth and Talitha

Miriam, Barth & Regina, Christmas morning

Librarian

Blake, a perfect height to sit on for a ride around the block

Amiel and Mom

Mim with Elaine, lifelong friend

Mim and Ann, best friends

Future writer!

Mom volunteering in Bangladesh

All of us together

Now

Chapter Thirteen

My Mother Is a Mountaineer

My mother has climbed Mount Everest.
She summited by way of the Southwest Face—
a brutal slog, but pluck and grit and a sturdy build
helped see her to the top.   Now an afternoon storm
has whitened out her view, and she is stranded
high above the South Col.   Only night will come down.
She sits in a snowdrift, waiting, as I set out
on my own ascent, base camp far below me
—Barth Landor

The last car my mother drove was a used, red convertible BMW.   What a great little car to zip around in compared to the former line-up of old duds: the VW van with a hole in the floor (our first car in Berea), the boring Fords and used Hondas.   Finally a car with some pizzazz.   Sadly, she didn't have it for long. She pulled over into a gas station one afternoon and did not emerge. A couple of hours passed before an attendant went over to look inside. He found my mother unconscious. When the ambulance arrived, she was soaking wet from her own sweat. She'd had a grand mal seizure.

Fortunately, the medication she was given following the grand mal helped control the seizures. She knew *exactly* which ones to take and when. She was meticulous about her doctor's appointments, which she got to by a community service van for some time, and help from her neighbors. She ordered her medications and diligently took them every day. She knew precisely which medicine was going to keep those seizures under control, and potentially save her life.

The medication does not prevent the seizures entirely and she still gets small ones, mild interruptions of the brain waves. She feels slightly nauseous, her mouth gets dry, and she knows a seizure is coming. When we are together now and she feels a seizure coming on, she will reach out to hold my hand, become very still, and get that far-away look in her eyes. It's a terrible feeling for her, knowing that it's coming, like a fast approaching train, but there's nothing she can do to stop it. The doctors told us in the beginning that eventually these seizures will chip away at her frontal lobes, which affect behavior, learning, and personality.

Yep.

However, for a long time she took care of herself. She lived in Berea on her own for about 13 years after her brain surgery. She walked to church. She met friends for coffee. She continued renting out rooms in her home. She formed bonds with her renters. She walked across the street, along the tree-lined path through the college campus, and on into downtown Berea to go to the library or do her shopping.

And she did what she's always loved best—she travelled. She flew to Chicago often, visiting my brother and her granddaughters.

The farthest she flew during that period was all the way to Romania. I had met Billy Woodward during my Peace Corps service there, and we were nearing the end of my first year. My mom was itching to visit, and I wanted her to meet the man I was going to marry. There was nothing that was going to stop her.

Boy, did we ever have a goofy, fun time during those two weeks in Romania. We picked her up at the airport and Billy knew which woman was my mother the moment she stepped off that plane. A blond, older woman beaming at me. He remembers how spry she was and how, when he put out his hand to shake hers, she gave him a big hug.

My mom stayed with me for a week in the small town where I was teaching and where I had a small apartment with a double bed that we shared. She got a kick out of the students. She came to a few of my English classes—in an unheated classroom the size of a large closet—and listened to a couple of kids standing in front of the room practicing their English. Two male students were role-playing a scene in a courtroom. Instead of saying, Yes sir, your honor, one of the boys mistakenly said, I love you, your honor. My mom giggled for days over that.

I think because I had already been in Eastern Europe for a full year by the time she arrived, I was used to seeing things that I would not see at home: livestock on the streets, Roma encampments, crowded buses with passengers carrying chickens, smelling like garlic, and squeezing in next to strangers.

The other cultural idiosyncrasy I was used to was the fear of a current and the conviction that a breeze of any kind could make a person sick, or an already sick person sicker, so that it was no longer unusual for me to see people wrapped in layers covering their ears and neck, or plugging their ears with cotton in a moving vehicle. The director of the middle school, a very distinguished-looking man, had invited us over for lunch; only we didn't know he had stayed home from school that day because of a cold. When we appeared at his apartment, he answered the door wearing a fluffy, pink hat covering his ears completely, the kind of hat a little girl might wear on a snowy day. His neck was wrapped in a matching pink scarf. I suppose to him it didn't matter what it looked like, as long as his neck and ears were covered! The bemused look in my mother's eyes stayed there all through lunch, as she tried to take the conversation seriously, and did not leave until we were well out of hearing range and she could laugh her head off at the spectacle he created.

We got to travel with Billy, too, during those two weeks. Even back then there were glimpses of the compassion that he was to show her years later; that same affection that he displayed toward her on that trip is still present over a decade later.

From Bucharest, we boarded a train for Sanaia, Romania, a beautiful town in the hills with a nineteenth century castle. Catching that train, though, was an adventure in itself. Billy got a sudden craving for a hamburger just minutes before the train was to depart, and there was a McDonald's right there in the station.

He took off. Romanians, at the time, were not known for their good customer service. From the platform where we stood, we could see Billy through the glass windows standing in line, waiting and waiting. I was watching the clock and *man*, I kept thinking, that train is going to pull out of the station any minute. We'll miss it if he doesn't get that damn hamburger. Come *on*, Billy. Come *on*. Finally! He grabbed his bag of food just as the whistle started blowing. And the train slowly started moving. *Run!* I am screaming to Billy, *Run!* I grab hold of my mom's hand and our luggage. We are running down the platform trying to get in front of an open train car. Billy catches up while strangers are holding out their arms for us. We are somehow hoisted into a car along with our luggage and I am laughing so hard by now I cannot catch my breath. Welcome to Peace Corps, Mom!

I don't know if we got a seat or not on that train. I cannot remember, but my mother was the best sport imaginable. We did get a seat on a seven-hour bus ride back to my town after we visited Peace Corps friends on different trip, but we were sharing that two-person seat with another man. We didn't exchange one word with him, but my mom kept laughing about how well she was getting to know him.

When I decided at the end of the school year that I wanted to cut my two-year commitment to Peace Corps short so Billy and I could go home and get married, I learned that I was also no longer able to get the grant for my school to receive money for new toilets. I was crestfallen. When I told my mother this on the phone, she said she'd write a check herself. She was adamant. She gave the school two thousand dollars. Months later, we received a "Certificate for Miriam Landor" from the school. It was a great honor. They put a plaque up for her, too, right by those toilets.

When Billy and I moved to Peoria, Illinois, she often visited us flying from Cleveland to Chicago, and then taking the three-hour bus ride south. (No chickens in cages on those buses.) She and my sister Talitha, a lay-midwife at the time, were there at the birth of our first-born son. How she loved holding that baby, her first grandson. She couldn't get enough. When he was one, she bought him a book of the song "The Twelve Days of Christmas." Each page had little windows to open with delightful illustrations inside. They opened those windows together so often that it prompted the inscription: "To my beloved grandson, Ethan. To the many, many . . . many, many times I sang and you opened the 'doors.' May all the doors you open bring happiness. You are my joy. Love, Grandma Mimi." Several of those doors had to be taped back on—Ethan showed so much glee in opening them he tore them right off!

When Gabriel was born two years later, I decided I only wanted Billy and Talitha in the room during the birth. My mother was beginning to exhibit a level of anxiety that I didn't want in the birthing room. If she wanted, she could wait outside the room. That was fine. However, she inched her way into the room and stood behind a curtain. While I was in labor, I could see her feet under that curtain. Slowly, the feet started moving closer and closer to the front of the curtain. Every time I glanced at the curtain, her feet were closer to the front. Eventually she was standing by my bed holding my other hand. She couldn't listen to me suffer without giving me comfort. And she was a comfort. In the end, I was glad she was there.

At 72 years old, my mom was crawling around on the floor with my boys, singing to them, and insisting that she buy Ethan his first ice cream cone when he was two. With pride in her voice, she tells them now that it was *she* who taught them how to play tag. At eight and ten years old they both roll their eyes and Ethan says, "Grandma, you didn't *teach* us how to play tag!"

"Okay," I tell him, "maybe not *teach*. I get it—tag is an instinct. Someone chases you. You run. But she was definitely the first one who played it with you," I remind them. Her playfulness and sense of fun seemed to evolve to its fullest when her grandsons were little. She was still sprightly and nimble and full of energy.

But back in Berea on her own, she tripped over a crack in the sidewalk and had a bad fall. A neighbor went over to check up on her and found there was no food in her fridge. It sickened me. I remember feeling angry that she was not taking better care of herself. She was beginning to rely heavily on neighbors. Too heavily.

Rosemary was the best neighbor imaginable, however, and she lived right next door. It is funny how sometimes the right person appears in our lives at just the right time. Rosemary called my brother and me often, filling us in on the growing problems in my mother's life. She brought her food, she took her to the airport, she helped her when the upstairs bathroom flooded and she dragged furniture out of the basement when mold was discovered. She went far beyond what an ordinary neighbor would do. She was a true and compassionate friend. A woman with four children of her own, she volunteered around town and extended kindness to others with grace and humility. We thank our lucky stars that my mother ended up with her as a neighbor. It was a stroke of luck that over that period of time—several years, really—my mother had a woman by her side who helped deliver her safely into the next phase of her life.

Chapter Fourteen

The first move out of the house in Berea was to Talitha's farm in North Carolina. Barth flew to Berea from Chicago to help our mother pack tables, paintings, couches and chairs, dishes, little objects and photographs that would hang around the double-wide, a second home next to the farm house, to make it Miriam's home.

For a while, it worked. I think the realization that it was not going to work forever may have come when Tali walked in on my mother and saw the dining room table covered in pills. Piles here, piles there. Nothing in containers. She was starting to get deeply confused and not managing her meds well. Talitha took over administering the meds. But my mom talked to me on the phone frequently about not being able to get anywhere outside of the farm by herself. She was feeling despondent. She kept asking herself what she was doing living on a farm! There were all these goats, and she doesn't like goats! She wanted to be taking classes. She wanted to walk to the public library! And church!

The town was just too far away and even though plenty of arrangements were made for her to have more of an active life, she was not happy.

It was time for us to start looking around for a retirement home. At the time, it would not have occurred to us to invite my mother to live with us. Billy and I were just beginning our path in the Foreign Service and we were on our own complicated journey of leaving America to live abroad—with toddlers.

Everything about the retirement home in Evanston sounded ideal: coffee shops nearby, boutiques, libraries, a university, walking paths, family. Evanston, just north of Chicago, is a hub of cultural and urban activity. It was the perfect place for my mom to settle; plus, for now, she could afford it. She moved into her little two room suite there and she liked it a lot. At first.

Whether it was intentional or not, my mother started creating obstacles for this new living situation not to work. She became paranoid. The moment she started to misplace her belongings was the moment that led to her distrust of everyone in that building. She was afraid to leave her room for fear of someone coming in and taking her things. She laid traps to catch the culprit. She offered to *pay* the few friends she had in the building to stay in her room and guard her things while she went down to the dining room for a meal. Many of her belongings were still in Berea, in the house that was now being rented. She left many of her things in North Carolina, too. She was now living in two small rooms, which could accommodate only so much stuff. So when she went to reach for such and such a thing, it may not have been there. So where was it? Where is that sweater that I loved? Where is my butterfly brooch? Or my stacks of photo albums? *Where* are my things? Who is taking my *things*?

She called a detective. She blamed the retirement home staff. She talked to the other residents attempting to form some kind of rebellion against the staff. Then, we were told she had to leave.

We never told her this, but we didn't need to. She wanted out. She started to hate the place and she willingly agreed to look with us for a different home to live. We felt despair—it seemed like everything she had asked for was at her front door, but she was only able to focus on her missing belongings and her fear that more things would be taken. What she could not realize was what was really being taken from her was something that was completely out of anyone's control: her memory and her ability to see things rationally.

We did find another retirement home, but nothing changed. The situation merely worsened. Without our knowledge, private investigators were hired, shamelessly accepting payment. Again, she blamed the staff for taking her things. Or accused them of giving her the wrong medicine. I was living nearby during her year at this second retirement home, as Billy was serving a year in Afghanistan. I went to pick her up every weekend to come and stay with the boys and me. Once, I went back to her room to get her purse and found she had purposely put a plant by the door and spilled out some dirt to make it appear that someone had come into the room—knocking down the plant in the process of breaking in. Why was she doing this? Why was she setting the traps and hanging video cameras up in her room?

She could not admit that something was wrong with her and she desperately wanted proof that it wasn't her fault. Her brain did not allow for her to *see* that she had the problem. My mother was delusional. She had gone over the edge.

Chapter Fifteen

My mother became convinced that someone named Bill, maybe another resident, was coming into her room every day and moving things around. On one of the occasions I picked her up to spend the weekend with me, I asked her if she packed her slippers. In a mater-of-fact tone, she said, "Bill put them under the couch."

In a more hysterical tone, a few weekends later when I opened her door to get her she was holding up a man's tee shirt and screaming, "He left this in my closet!" Of course I recognized the shirt immediately. It was my husband's. She'd worn it at our house then packed it in her bag.

When I told her the mistake about the tee shirt, her face was defiant. She was determined to show me there was other proof. She went to her dresser and said, "Who put this here?" pointing to a paper clip. "There's a handkerchief there," jabbing the air in its direction. "I've never seen that in my life. This pillow has been moved. Now, why would I put that there? This picture frame—look! It's crooked!" Last weekend the teapot and the stapler were in the bathroom. "I wouldn't put those in the bathroom!" she yelled.

Sometimes when I was in the car with my children we'd drive by the other building my mother lived in for a year. My six-year-old reminded me, "That's where Grandma used to live!" He asked me why she doesn't live there anymore, so I told him.

"Grandma thought people were taking things from her room and she was bothering the other people who lived there," I said. "They told her she had to find another place to live." My boys listened quietly, absorbing the news about Grandma's decline.

Our challenge was trying to figure out how to respond to her delusions. It was no good just telling her she's the one moving things around, or hiding things. She wouldn't believe us, and she blamed us for not believing her. Installing a security camera did not help either. "The camera's no good. All I see is myself!"

During the summer that Billy was away, I took my mom and the kids to a week-long Unitarian camp for families. She was thrilled to be coming with us and was waiting with her bags packed in the lobby of her retirement home when I went to get her. I lifted up one of her bags to swing over my shoulder, and was halted mid-air by its weight. It felt like it was packed with bricks. "Mom!" I said. "What's in here?" I unzipped the bag and found her miniature, ceramic shoe collection, her brass statue of a girl on a swing, and lots of baggies filled with jewelry.

Somehow I managed to convince her to let me help her repack. We went upstairs, kids in tow, where we took out the statue, ceramic shoes, jewelry, and winter sweaters, and laid out more appropriate clothing for a week by the lake in the heat. She did not want to leave her things behind, but she did, and we finally got out the door and to the car.

Helping my children into the car, I looked up and saw my mom walking back toward her building. "Mom!" I shouted. She kept up her fast-paced stride. "Mom! STOP!" She ignored me. I ran up to her. "What are you doing?" I was beginning to feel frantic. We'd never get on the road. "I forgot to lock my door." She kept walking.

"No you didn't. I saw you lock it." She stopped. I couldn't remember if I had or hadn't, but it didn't matter. "I saw you lock it, Mom. Let's go." Relief swept over me when she finally complied.

I knew it was going to be a rough week, but I wanted to make this happen. I wanted her to enjoy herself, to forget about her living situation, to enjoy her grandchildren. I wanted to have some normal conversations with her where she was listening and responding and not always directing the conversation back to herself.

But I also knew I was going to have to swallow some pride. My mom's behavior—not just the delusion, but also the desperate need to feel wanted and loved—would show itself. And I was connected to her. She was connected to me. But it doesn't matter, I told myself. We are not the same person. However she behaves is not my responsibility. Besides, if there's a group that will understand odd behavior, it's this one.

During the introduction meeting on the first night of the camp, fifty of us sat in a large circle. Each person took a turn saying something about themselves. The words were moving closer to us. My mom's turn was fast approaching. Seconds before, she leaned over to me and whispered into my ear, "I'm going to embarrass you." She had that naughty, gleeful look in her eyes. I knew she'd stay true to her word. And she did. She told everyone her name, then stood up and inched herself closer to the center of the circle, and started singing.

"Oh, say can you see by the dawn's early light.

What so proudly we hailed at the twilight's last gleaming?"

Then she sat down. I looked up from the spot where I had fixed my eyes on the floor, daring myself to take it in. I saw people nod. I saw them thinking to themselves, Yeah, we've got an odd one on our hands, but it's okay. It's okay. We can go with that. These were Unitarians after all.

I struggled with her being there that week. She was upset that she couldn't make phone calls. She got up every night in our small cabin to turn on the light and look for things. She tossed and turned in her sleep. She ate an ice cream cone just before dinner and—no longer hungry—watched us regretfully as we ate a healthy meal. She was like a child who needed constant supervision. The saddest part about the week was that she couldn't hear most of the conversations, having lost her hearing aids the week before.

Still, there were moments during the week when my mom was just my mom. There were times when she appeared totally normal and herself, her true self. Like when she lay in the hammock with the boys and read them a story. Another such moment was when the group was sharing thoughts aloud, and one more time, my mother took her turn. I stared at the floor again, preparing myself for another—I don't know what. How was she going to embarrass me this time? She stood up.

"I'd like to say how proud I am of my son-in-law, Regina's husband," she said, turning to look at me. I really think this is what she was trying to say the first time around, with her patriotic song. Now, she was able to find the words to explain. "He's in Afghanistan right now making a sacrifice for us all. He is there for us, for all of us. I'm proud of him, as we all should be." Then she took her seat.

In that moment, she'd come out of the woods. Her words were eloquent and lucid. She spoke earnestly and compassionately. It was my mom, come back. I squeezed her hand when she sat back down, and she squeezed mine.

Chapter Sixteen

A factor that played heavily into Billy's decision to serve in Afghanistan now in his career was my mother. We knew that if he was going to stay in the Foreign Service at some point he was going to have to serve in a CPC—a Critical Priority Country. It would be an unaccompanied post, so the boys and I would have to stay home. After two years in Serbia, we'd now get to spend a full year with my mother in the States. It was excellent timing.

I was with my mother so often during that year, taking her to her doctor's appointments, making sure she was safe in her retirement home, trying to secure her happiness and comfort, that I burst into tears on the phone with Talitha when I told her that our next assignment was in South Asia, for four years. How could I leave my mother?

That conversation occurred shortly after our visit from Raenette and Charlene, which got me thinking. So I said to Tali on the phone after the tears, Maybe I'll talk to Billy about her coming with us. She thought it was an excellent idea, and sighed along with me about the relief that we would all feel if that were to happen.

It was going to be a process, but Billy saw it as the next, natural progression. And that's when he said that if it were his mother, he'd want to do the same.

We got the ball rolling.

And then Billy had an R&R. He was home and we were all together, planning our future in Bangladesh with my mother in tow. She was jittery with excitement, but maybe it all sounded too good to be true and she didn't quite believe us—that she was really going to live with us. That we were going to take care of her and that she would no longer have to live in that dreaded retirement home. That she was going to travel with us on a plane going overseas and that we were going to have this adventure together and that she was going to be included. Maybe it all sounded to her like a fairy tale.

Around the same time that our new plans were unfolding, my mother had the misfortune of going to a doctor who drastically changed the type of medication she was taking and the dosage. She suddenly was not walking correctly. Where she had been walking steadily a few days before, she was now starting to wobble. Something was not right.

Perhaps it was a combination of circumstances: anxiety around the upcoming move overseas, her not quite believing that it was really going to happen, the change in her medication. Whatever triggered the blow, it turned out to be explosive, and we were just lucky that Billy was home to be there for support. My mother had a full-blown psychotic breakdown.

It really began the night before, with her not being able to walk properly. Then, in the morning, she started accusing me of lying to her—saying that it wasn't really true that we were taking her with us. She kept following me around the house aggressively demanding that I tell her it's not really true.

Her sister called and my mom started talking with her, but suddenly she was talking gobbledygook and Ann couldn't understand what she was saying. I took the phone from my mom—struggled to get it out of her hands—and Ann was crying. I told Ann we're taking my mom to the hospital. I was thanking my lucky stars the whole time that Billy was there. But my mom refused to get into the car. And we realized it was pointless. With the fight she was putting up, we'd probably have an accident on the way over.

Her pugnacious behavior continued even when the ambulance and police arrived. We were in the driveway and Billy and I were told to go into the house. My mother refused to comply. She was yelling at the officers. They finally got her on to a stretcher and strapped her down. We followed the ambulance and by the time we got to the hospital, my mother was thrashing around and starting to foam at the mouth.

The nurses gave her a sedative, which calmed her down. During the whole ordeal of people coming and going, of her yelling at nurses and doctors, of everyone trying to figure out how to deal with her, a caseworker came into the room to ask my mom a series of questions. She was calmer by now and more lucid and able to respond.

Marry Me Stop

The caseworker was a large woman with short hair, and had a frank, open expression. I liked her the moment I saw her. She was kind. She had a whole list of questions for my mom, to test her mind. Questions like, Date of birth, What year is it, Who is the president. And more personal questions, like, Do you own a gun. My mom didn't hear her and said, A gub? This was straight out of a Woody Allen movie. The woman looked at me and as tense as I was, I was smiling and she was trying not to smile but couldn't help herself, and my mom then understood the question and said, A gun? Why would I own a *gun*? And she looked at this woman like she was crazy and my mom even started to laugh until we were all laughing. The caseworker showed such compassion. She talked gently to my mom and looked directly at her and then out in the hallway, she said to me, This is why I love my job. People like her.

Our lives at the time were like pieces of a scattered puzzle that somehow came together and formed a perfect story. During the same week that my mother was in the hospital, we moved out of our rental and into our new condo. There was only one bed left in the hospital nearest our new condo, and it was secured immediately for my mom. Had we still been in our rental, we would have had a long drive back and forth. Billy was home for three full weeks, enabling me to visit my mother late at night. The best we could do in response to the negligent doctor who put her on the wrong meds, in lieu of filing a lawsuit, was to find a better doctor, and that doctor happened to work in the hospital where she was admitted.

She was being monitored and her head was hooked up to the monitoring equipment and she looked like she was only half alive when Billy came in to see her. I saw his mouth twitch downward and he said he thought it was time to call the family. Within that first week, the neurologist said it was too early to tell if she was going to be okay. It was obvious that for my mom, Bangladesh was out.

She refused to take her medicine. She fought the nurses so that the only thing left to do was to give her the meds through a tube up her nose and down into her throat and to strap her down again because she kept trying to pull out the tubes.

She was not making any sense. During my visits she was talking gibberish to imaginary people who were not there. She had to be helped to get to the bathroom. She was in giant diapers! I went to see her every day, and she still couldn't walk. Once, she was arguing with a nurse late at night when I walked into the room. Her wrists were tied down. She didn't know what was happening to her. She heard my voice—a voice she recognized at last—and turned to me and called out my name with such urgency and relief. I convinced the nurses to untie her because I was there and I would stay with her and make sure she did not pull at the tubes. Then I sat with her and soothed her and lay down in the bed with her, holding her hands at her side until she went to sleep.

Her meds were all out of whack. The doctor was trying to stabilize her and each day we visited he told us that sometimes patients come out of this kind of breakdown and sometimes they do not.

Marry Me Stop

Miriam did. After ten days, she started acting a bit like her old self again. She was able to eat, and she started taking her medicine again. She was finally released from the hospital and her sister flew in to help care for her. She started walking normally again. And then she started talking normally. Her meds seemed to be in balance. We were leaving in six weeks. Was Bangladesh really out? Maybe not. Maybe she really has it in her after all.

The family and I started talking again like it was a possibility. Then we started talking about it like it was a reality. We started closing down her life at the retirement home. Then we started packing. It was really happening. We were taking my mother with us to Dhaka, Bangladesh.

During that year, Billy got a medal in Afghanistan. The boys received a medal from the State Department for being without their daddy for a year. I jokingly wondered out loud, Where the heck is *my* medal? And then at our going-away party, Raissa presented me with one. On the front of the medal it said, "Woman of Valor." I wore that around my neck, hoping against odds that on this new journey into the unknown—of a new country, of my mother moving in with us—that I would be worthy of my medal and that my courage would not fail me.

Chapter Seventeen

My mother had this image in her mind of Billy leading all of us on this great expedition, through the various airports, down the runways, and on to our final destination. In her mind, Billy was the torchbearer, our guiding light who would see us all the way over the ocean, over Europe and over deserts, and into the tropical land of South Asia.

She was off by only a little bit. I did a lot of the leading, too. But she was completely right in that she followed us every step of the way. Every time I turned around to count the troops there were two boys and one grandma wheeling suitcases and not falling behind. When I looked at her and gave her the thumbs-up, she'd smile and give me the thumbs-up back. When I'd say, Are you okay? She'd say, I'm okay are *you* okay? We kept a careful eye on her because she didn't know which way was up. Or out. I swear, when she was being searched in a tiny booth, she couldn't find the exit curtain. Even the boys took care of her. On the plane, without noticing that I was watching, my six-year-old reached over and helped her with her seatbelt.

Oh, Dhaka. A most foreign land. It was very hard to breathe when we first arrived. And I don't mean because of the smell of the open sewers or the pollution or the dust in our noses. It was just hard to catch our breath and assess where we were.

It felt like our quiet and steady family had been placed inside a giant, spinning kaleidoscope of color and clamorous sound and all we could do to keep our grip on some semblance of reality was to hold each other's hand.

For one, the chaos. The movement of traffic is a world unto itself. It's a dirty, dusty, grimy machine that only functions because of the laws that are not adhered to. It's kept oiled not by a list of instructions but by an unwritten code of movement that only the very brave attempt to break.

As we drove away from the airport on that first day, the day we arrived, I felt such bleakness outside the car window that I didn't even want to look up. When I forced myself to do so, to take it in, all I saw was a world that was so unpromising and dire it was all I could do to keep from crying and hold my breath and hope that my kids and my mom had the strength of character to bear what they saw, too.

The van that was transporting us from the airport to our temporary apartment was at a standstill. As far as I could tell, there were no traffic lanes and there was no space between the cars. The cars were inching forward, like a giant mass of metal on a concrete plane with few gaps in between. If I could put my hand out the window, I would be able to touch the car next to ours. How would an ambulance get past? I was told never to put my hand out the window. Don't ever give money to a beggar from your car window. The car could easily be surrounded.

Where to look? Where not to look? People without limbs were tapping on our windows. Men without hands. People with deformities unseen by us before were pleading with their eyes through our windows, grotesquely hunched and deformed. Old men, blind, hunched over, with canes. Women without teeth, tapping. Women with naked babies, asleep on their shoulders. I told my mother to look away. She should not have to see this, I told myself. The sadness of this scene—were we right to bring my mother here? The babies were naked and the women were incessantly tapping, tapping. My mother and I locked eyes and I saw the confusion and sadness in her face. I think my kids were in a state of numbed shock. I told them to look away, too. Look away from the helpless and maimed. Look away. What are we teaching them in this moment? It was a rough beginning. There were plenty more traffic standstills to come.

One of the most frightening and exotic things that I saw during our very first week in Dhaka was a giant hornet's nest perched between two branches of a tree right outside our apartment building. Another name for the occupants of this strange-looking habitat is the killer hornet, and I stood a good distance away and watched them coming and going from their bulbous, hanging home. The story the guard told me becomes the stuff of legends. A kid walking past it tempted it with his shoe. He threw his shoe high up into the trees upsetting the nest and creating a reaction that caused a ripple of pain. A swarm flew out and people went running. And the swarm followed. I stood on our screen-covered balcony and imagined that scene in the street below, a dark, dangerous, angry cloud flying in pursuit of the culprit, attacking whichever pour soul happened to be nearby. We missed the spectacle by about a week.

My first impressions of Bangladesh, along with the disheartening ride from the airport, were formed from the windows and screen-covered balcony of our apartment. I stared out that window for a long time during those first few days. The laborers looked like a colony of ants, a silent, dark path forming a moving, straight line, one following the other, carrying what looked like twice the weight of their own bodies on top of their heads. I didn't know where they were going with their loads and I didn't know where they went once their loads were delivered. I only knew that there were a lot of them. Many, many of them. Inside this industrious social network were the female workers sitting on their haunches on the ground below, hammering bricks. Above them all, bright green parrots perched on bamboo scaffolding. The hornet's nest was suspended on a branch nearby.

If we are going to live in this country, I decided early on, we are going to be brave and the only way to be brave is to face up to it and the only way to face up to it is to get a sense of where we are and the only way to do that is to enter it and look it straight in the eyes. We're going on a walk. Boys, put on your shoes.

It was the end of the monsoon season and humid. Step outside and almost immediately you feel the sweat trickle down your spine. We took baby-steps at first because we didn't know where we were going, but there was a park across the road from our temporary apartment. The paved path went around a small pond. Three times around made up a mile. Little brown boys were bathing in the murky water. They splashed each other and waved at us. A man in a long, checkered cloth wrapped around his waist carefully and discreetly took it off and he bathed himself, too, scrubbing his body with a rag and some soap. We heard the whack of a hard ball and saw a boy swing a cricket bat with full force. A playground slide in some dirt was so steep and unsafe-looking, a sheet of buckled metal; we didn't even need to tell our kids not to play on it.

Every day that first week we went to the park. It was Eid, the end of Ramadan. There was a celebration. The month of fasting was over and everyone could at last eat during the day-time hours. We saw people clustered around little carts with large bags of puffed rice. A man chopped chili peppers, added some spices and a little chopped cucumber, tomatoes, and onions, mixed it with the puffed rice, which turned a mustard color from the spices, and put it in a little paper cup for a few cents in return. We stood by the cart as a family and watched the exchange. Children wore festive, colorful clothing. Women wrapped in multi-colored saris stood very close together in groups under the tropical trees, the palms and the coconuts. And they surrounded us as we walked past them in our western clothes. We were an oddity. We were unique. We were fascinating, much more interesting than the festival going on around them. *We* were the festival.

I got used to it but I didn't like it.

Marry Me Stop

When you're in the Foreign Service, an instant family is formed by the other expats who happen to be in the same city as you. You see members of your newly acquired family almost everywhere you go: the clubs, the doctor's office, the grocery store, the embassy, the school, the balls, the tailor's, and the countless, all-year-round birthday parties for kids and adults. At a coffee morning my mother and I attended while Billy was now at work and the boys now in school, someone who was about to depart post began speaking about her time in Dhaka. She said that people always say that you cry when you arrive and you cry when you leave. And she was about to leave and she was crying.

I could not envision myself in her shoes. Why would I cry about leaving this stinking mess? It was still really scary to go outside, mostly because of the traffic. The cycle rickshaws are fast, and they line the streets and whiz by and you wonder how you survive every single dusty step you take. It seemed there was no escaping the open garbage bins and open sewers that reeked of an unbearable foulness. There is so much *trash*. The edge of the lake, we noticed, was an unnatural blue—dye dumped in the water from one of the many factories. And there was no way to escape the noise of construction—hammering, banging, drilling, pounding—and the noise of the blaring car horns. As a warning to other cars in an intersection, drivers lean on their horns. Stop signs don't exist.

The one solid bit of comfort that I experienced during those first weeks of being in Dhaka while Billy, Ethan, and Gabriel were out of the house was seeing my mom right there in the living room with me. There she was—my mom! I did not experience a sense of loneliness like I did during our first posting in Belgrade. I had a companion that I'd known all of my life and we were sharing this new experience together. I was vigilant about giving her meds to her. The last thing in the world we wanted was a psychotic breakdown in Dhaka.

We hired an *ayah* right away, a nanny who cooked and cleaned and watched the kids and my mom if I needed to go out. We bought a car from a departing diplomat. We found a driver who would become so essential to our comfort and well-being in Dhaka, Mahabub soon became practically a member of our family. We wondered how we would survive without the two of them.

Our *ayah* walked us through the cavernous maze of the market to help us buy food; our driver took us to the embassy to meet Billy for lunch and to the hospital where we met a neurologist for my mother who helped her adjust her medicine again. The doctor had been trained in the States and that was a blessed relief.

We moved into our new apartment, a sunny, large space with a suite on one end for my mother and two *en suite* bedrooms on the other end for the four of us. It was ideal and it had a large, sliding door and a balcony with a view of—what else?—a construction site. But the interior felt luxurious because of the layout and the light, and with plants and our things about to arrive, we would make it our home. It was a delightful respite to come back to after trudging around outside. One thing was needed to enhance the overall joyful feeling of the space: curtain tiebacks and paint. I chose the happiest shades of color I know—orange—and painted a few of the walls. Home at last.

Chapter Eighteen

How was our heroine, Miriam, doing in all of this? How was she faring in this sea of unfamiliarity? In the humidity, the foul smells, the traffic, the beggars, the potholes, the dust, the pollution, and the monsoons?

Our Miriam just kept rising to the occasion and did not disappoint. She was faring just fine. She never did get sick, for one. We spent half the year keeling over a toilet and she sailed right on through. She followed me everywhere and was happy to do so. She did not complain. Every now and then she'd lift up her head and notice things, taking stock of her surroundings. She commented on the laborers, and saw how work that would be done with heavy machinery in the States is done by hand here, digging up an entire road to lay pipes, for example. She noticed the young men standing around on the street corners, at the tea stalls, unemployed. And in the comfort of our air-conditioned minivan, she marveled at the traffic and how few accidents occur. My mother was a genuine trooper and I loved having her with me.

Regina Landor

I love having her with me partly because she forms a kind of protective wall around me when I'm outside. She creates a sensation whenever we go for a walk. It's a curious thing. Everyone stares at her, and she's oblivious to it. Groups of men stop chatting with each other and follow us with their eyes as we walk past. Men at the tea stalls stop drinking, hold their little glasses of tea in their hands and silently watch her. Her head is bent down; her eyes are fixed on each and every step she takes, and she doesn't notice the men. I surmise that Bangladeshis are not used to seeing elderly white women. Perhaps she is the very first elderly white woman they have ever seen. Perhaps, also, they have a reverence for her. I sense a deep respect—for her and for me in that I am caring for her.

I tell her as we walk, "Mom, people are delighted to see you. Everyone stares at you!" She's definitely shrunk over the years. My eyes are level with hers now, and I'm five-foot-four, but still she tells me, "That's because I'm five-foot-eight, blue-eyed and blond."

Yeah, but aren't they supposed to be checking out *me* too, the gorgeous redhead? No one's really checking out me.

In the early days, she wanted to go out walking alone. I tell her that would be impossible, and we argue. She wants to be independent. She doesn't understand how it would be unsafe, how dangerous the traffic is, how she'd get lost and never find her way back alone.

So I walk with her. I hold her arm and guide her. I lead her down the street toward the park or the store or the club and back again to our apartment. We walk together and come back and stand in front of our apartment building and I say to her, "Mom, do you know where our apartment building is?" She looks one way, then the other way, and every other way except right in front of her. She has no idea.

She says to me, "I'm *so* glad you come with me on these walks, Regina." As if she'd be out here walking around by herself.

Once she fell flat on her face over a pile of branches on the sidewalk. I was not quick enough to catch her. Men standing around rushed up to her to help. A rickshaw was immediately by our side. She only suffered a few scrapes on her knees that time; but now I'm more vigilant about holding her arm when we walk so that she won't trip over the many obstructions in our path: the stray dogs asleep on the sidewalk, the holes, the rubble, the trash. And it takes an effort to avoid the dangling rubber electric cords that are bunched up above us running along the length of the sidewalk, a stray noose here and there just at neck level.

A man stops us outside our apartment building. "Your mother?" he asks me. I tell him, Yes. "How old?" he asks, smiling. "One hundred?" No! Only 78. Another man smiles and says, "Your mother? You lucky. My mommy and daddy die." He turns to my mom and says in a loud voice, "How are you, Ma'am? You ok? How Bangladesh? You like Bangladesh?" He has a broad smile, missing teeth and red lips and teeth from the betel leaf he's been sucking on. It's impossible for us not to smile in return.

When you're in the Foreign Service and moving to a new city every couple of years, you spend at least the first six months, if not the entire time you're there, doing one thing: amassing information. We learned pretty quickly the whereabouts of the nearest spa. *Hello? Priorities?* Manicures, pedicures, shoulder rubs, and back massages are the way of life for the leisurely, unemployed woman here; I could take my mom to the salon once a week if she wanted, or more. La Femme, a spa for women, is right down the road from us and it's become a weekly routine to take her. If I am busy, Mahabub will take her and wait for her on the street below. She loves getting a bargain—and walking out of there having only spent ten dollars, it is the best deal in town.

Walks in the park, trips to the salon, going to the American Club—one of the few open, green spaces nearby with a pool, restaurant, and park—we were broadening our horizons outside of our apartment. And we were meeting people. But I was always with my mom and it wasn't always easy. She can't hear well, she repeats herself, and she asks the same questions. I was hesitant about bringing her everywhere with me. I was worried that when I walked into a room people might be inwardly groaning. It felt awkward for me at first, taking her to a wine and cheese party where I was afraid she was going to trip over a rug, knock something over, spill something, create a scene.

But people didn't seem to be thinking those things that I imagined. I kept meeting more and more people—women and men—who were genuinely kind and always greeted Miriam in a warm, friendly way. No one seemed to be bothered if she repeated herself. People were gracious when they saw her. She was being included and this outreach helped me feel more comfortable. I didn't need to be embarrassed about anything. This is who she is. This is where she is in her life right now. So I decided, to hell with it. I'm including her. (Except, Billy and I reserve one night a week for ourselves: our date night.) The first big event we took my mom to was the Marine Ball, the annual birthday bash to honor the Marines. She put on her one cocktail dress, drank wine, danced and we all had a great time. Everyone welcomed her.

There was one friend in particular whom I met soon after we moved into our new apartment building that helped ease the transition of having my mother live with us more than any other and that was Gina. Her warm spirit and humor allowed me to more easily accept my mother's near-constant presence by my side.

Gina's husband, Louie, was with the Department of Justice and they and their two little girls were only in Dhaka for a one-year assignment. I felt an immediate connection and I knew almost right away that it was going to be a sad day when they left. Friends come and go so frequently; the only thing to do is to appreciate every good moment you have with them. And we did and loved every conversation and every good laugh. It was Louie who videotaped my mom out on that dance floor at the Marine Ball.

My mom has this nightgown that she's had for years. It's a long, knitted cotton dress, really. She likes to tell me that it really *is* a dress and sometimes she'll say that if she wants, she can wear it outside because it's really a dress. But mom, I tell her, you've worn it as a nightgown for so long, it's not really a dress anymore. It's your nightgown!

Louie encouraged her every time he came over and she was in that nightgown. "Miriam, that's a nice dress!" He said it every time he saw her in it. "Miriam! You're wearing that dress that I like!"

Gina thought my mother reminded of her of her own grandmother. She was always so genuinely kind to her, asking her how she's doing and really meaning it. She would throw her head back and laugh hard at comments my mother made. When we were in Gina's apartment, she was showing my mother and me a painting she had done. It was of a group of stick figures that she did with her left hand, blindfolded! She wanted to see what she could create—and then she painted them. It's a child-like and delightful piece. My mom took one look at it and said, "I have some friends who look like that." Gina laughed so hard. Her laughter at my mother's comments made me laugh and appreciate her wit even more.

My mom still surprises me with her quick-witted one-liners. I think many elderly people get lumped into a category, into the realm of history even while they are still very much alive. They have slowed down, but they are still there. I see this sometimes when we are in a group setting and the chatter is rapid and my mom is trying very hard to follow along. I see her wanting to jump in and participate. I see the words forming on her mouth, but she's not quick enough, and the subject changes before she's had the opportunity to add her two cents, her joke, her connection to what was being said.

Despite the new hearing aids, she can't hear well and I believe she's confused between not being able to hear and not understanding the language. She's told people that her biggest problem here is the language. On our way to a party she said, I hope I'll be able to understand. But mom, everyone will be speaking English! I said. It's got to be a somewhat lonely world when everyone in a room bursts out laughing and you don't know why.

One-on-one usually works best, especially if the other person is willing to meet her at her own pace. It does take time and it takes patience, but I always feel a rush of gratitude when someone stops for a few moments to acknowledge her. Like, when my friend Olivia was sitting next to her at a table with a group of others and she turned to my mom and said that she's tired and wants to take a nap. "I'm taking a nap right now with my eyes open," my mom says. A pause, then Olivia erupted into peals of laughter.

Chapter Nineteen

I struggled in Dhaka in the beginning with the simple pleasures of dining out, or a shoulder rub, and a pedicure, knowing that there are people starving in the streets below me. The shock of seeing a man lying prostrate on the sidewalk with a begging bowl by his side is not easy to ignore. As I sit in my air-conditioned minivan I wonder if the man who's lying down in the gutter is still breathing until I see his ribs slowly moving up and down. And I always wonder where those children without shoes will get their next meal. I wonder about the constant pain in their stomachs.

I had a hard time truly enjoying myself in that lounge chair getting a pedicure at the Nordic Club in those early days. I was sitting in an outdoor patio next to an expat from Canada. I expressed aloud some of the guilt I was feeling. She said to me in that moment, "Life is hard here. It's hard on your emotions and it's hard on your feet. You need to give yourself a break. Enjoy it."

Marry Me Stop

My mom hated not being able to give. We could not hand money out of our car window. Plus, we were told that the beggars around the traffic circle are the victims of an enormous mafia, and that there's one guy at the top of this ring that collects the money and in turn, "helps" the beggars. I didn't want to contribute to that. But we could hand out fruit. That was her idea—to have fruit in the car to give. So, occasionally, we did that. And we stocked the glove compartment with peanuts to give to kids when we were stuck in the traffic circle.

We also learned of a street school in the slums where we could volunteer and teach an English class. I set up a day of the week to visit and bring my mom. At first, she was eager to participate. But soon her eagerness turned into anxiety, and practically despair, thinking she needed to plan, to teach the kids how to read, to prepare for lessons. She wouldn't listen to me when I told her that was nonsense—she didn't need to do anything! Just come along for the ride. Watch me. Read them a story if you'd like. No pressure. She would not listen to me and she ended up feeling bad about herself each and every time we went. The brooding could last for days; I finally gave up bringing her altogether.

The desire to do something to help the hungry street kids bonded us with two other newbies who had arrived on the scene at the same time we did. I met Priscilla at the same coffee morning with the woman who cried about leaving Dhaka. And Gina lived three floors above us in our apartment building.

We met and talked about what it is that we could do—what is that *something* that we can do—instead of just ignoring the massive problem of hunger in the streets? Probably not a lot, but finding a way to give some food to some of the kids would be better than doing nothing at all. We learned of a school in the slums, and we started buying bananas for the kids. Then we expanded to boiled eggs, some fresh fruits and raw vegetables, carrots and cucumbers, and roasted peanuts. We brought the food to the school, and we learned of a few other schools and brought food there. We brought in soap and made sure the kids had clean hands before eating their snack and donations came in from Facebook friends and Rotary Clubs at home and Gina came up with a name for our little organization: Thrive.

My mom tagged along, and Priscilla and Gina always made a point of including her. She washed the kids' hands. That was her job. And she loved it. She would say, "The kids love to be touched! It's so important—that connection, to touch them and to hold their hands!" We started to gather volunteers for our operation and Priscilla honed in on my mother's words and drew attention to that during some of our volunteer meetings, as a way of including my mom. My mom was offered a task in Dhaka and it made her feel important. She was participating in a good deed and it was meaningful.

It's easy to become numb, not to notice anymore. Or not to care. I am certainly guilty of that. I don't care all the time and I sometimes ignore what's around me if I want to get on with the issues of my own life—raising my own kids, helping my mom, buying the groceries, being there for Billy, writing.

Thrive gave our lives a purpose here, and helped us to care. When I sometimes wondered what the heck I was doing in Dhaka, Thrive gave me my answer. It also raised awareness and brought many people into the slums that would not otherwise have ever gone, including some Bangladeshis. Expats started to learn about Thrive and we began to get more volunteers who wanted to help. Going into the slums was usually a peaceful experience, too. There's less noise because of no cars. But there's hustle and bustle and little shops and tea stalls and people rolling out dough to make round, flat bread, and little barber shops, pharmacies, corrugated tin roofs, one-room homes and school houses, and extreme poverty—it is a sprawling village and it's only a few blocks from our apartment. We spent a couple of mornings a week there, and my mom was always happy to help. Not just happy, but grateful. It filled her with gladness, seeing those kids smiling at her, washing their little hands, and being treated with respect and fondness.

Some mornings she woke up and the first thing she'd ask me is, "Are we washing hands today?"

Other mornings she'd wake up looking like a train wreck. Her face was withdrawn, she didn't greet me—only a silent, angry presence. One thing that was clear from the get-go was that I never knew how my mother would wake up in the mornings. Sometimes she was cheerful. Many times, she was despondent.

Side effects of the anti-psychotic drug were back pain and nightmares. But she had to be on the drug. She despised it mostly, we believed, because of the stigma attached to it. But she was not going to live with us without taking the drug. We didn't know what a psychotic breakdown would look like in Bangladesh. We didn't trust the ambulance service or the hospitals.

We also didn't entirely trust Miriam. Living in Dhaka was not the first time my mother talked about knives, or doing something dangerous. When Ethan was an infant, she had a premonition that she was going to do something to hurt him, so she cancelled her trip to see us at that time.

Now, in Dhaka, she started talking to Billy and me about her fear of knives again and how she wanted us to hide the ones in the kitchen. Billy asked her questions about her fear. "Do you have thoughts of hurting yourself?" She didn't think so. "Do you have thoughts of hurting others?" She wasn't sure. When we asked her specifically if she had thoughts of hurting the boys, she said, "I would never hurt them!" And we believed that she wouldn't do anything intentionally, but we were not going to take any chances. At night, we put a chair in the hallway between her bedroom and our end of the apartment. Then we found a psychiatrist.

The Muslim psychiatrist at the hospital wore layers of clothes and a scarf wrapped tightly around her whole head, revealing only her face. It was an open, kind face and the biggest difference between the psychiatrists that my mother had seen in the States— aside from their genders—was that this one was kind and looked at my mother when she asked her a question. The doctors that she saw in Chicago never addressed their questions to her, only to my brother who was with her, and never looked her in the eye. It made her feel diminished, if not entirely invisible. The doctor in Dhaka listened to her. But she also raised the dosage of the anti-psychotic drug. She put her on an anti-depressant, too, to help the despondency and the anxiety that were ever-present.

She continued to complain about the medicine, but at least for a while she stopped talking knives.

Chapter Twenty

When did life start to click and feel like we were all in balance? Was it when we started to feel more at home in our cool apartment to which we returned from the heat and the dust of the day? Was it because of the Marine Ball and the excitement of having a hand-tailored gown? Or the school where the boys had superb teachers and an exciting curriculum? It helped enormously that we found doctors at Apollo who had been trained in the States. It helped that we were making friends and that those friends helped jump-start our new living situation with my mother with an acceptance of her that fueled our own acceptance. Many factors played into our gelling as a family and becoming not just the four of us and Grandma, but the five of us. We became one family.

And like any family, we laughed and we fought, we loved and we hugged, we were compassionate and we were short-tempered. My own goal of being courageous and accepting of my mother waxed and waned. There were times when it seemed impossible to control my fury. I would get unreasonably angry at her behavior. There were times I exploded and just needed to run away. But there was nowhere to run. I wanted to jump in my car, roll down the windows, turn on the music, and drive down a highway for miles and miles with nowhere to go. Not possible.

I had to deal with it because it's what I said I would do. It was my personal challenge, to treat my mother's decline with grace. But sometimes grace just walked out the door. Where the hell was grace when I needed it the most? Sometimes, I just couldn't do it.

In the evenings she was sweet and loving and funny and kind, but then something could happen to reverse the mood.

We hosted a party at Priscilla's for the volunteers for Thrive. We showed a slideshow and my mom was featured in a lot of the pictures, smiling and washing the kids' hands. I felt proud of her. We laughed with our friends in the car on the way home. I was glad we took my mom out. She was happy to be out, too.

When we got home she retreated to her bedroom, but then came out in her nightgown and said that her necklace was gone. Here we go again. My husband and I rolled our eyes. We were in for a night of it.

"What are the chances that you've hidden it?" my husband asked her. "It was taken," she said. "I'm sure of it." My husband was upset. It felt like our nice evening had just been shattered by this nonsensical, mad game.

She always says that she'll give a hundred dollars to the charity of our choice if we find her jewelry. "You're up to 600 dollars!" my husband shouted from the couch. It's actually probably higher.

Marry Me Stop

My mother, wringing her hands, her face dark with anxiety, paced the apartment. I went into her room and began the search, pulling out drawers, rifling through her closets. I knew that if we didn't find it we'd potentially be up all night—or worse, she'd wake us up in the middle of the night.

I could not find it in me to be compassionate. I was tired. This was the weekend and I just wanted to enjoy it, be at home, and be peaceful. It wasn't gonna happen. The longer I searched her bedroom, the more aggressive my actions became. I was pushing aside her clothes, shaking her comforter up and down, and pulling down the suitcases. God, where the hell was that goddamn necklace? I was swearing. She was shocked and appalled. This was her long, silver necklace with the mother Mary and Jesus pendant, after all. The more shocked and appalled she acted at my behavior, the angrier I became until I finally threw up my hands and quit.

I put her medicine on the counter, told my husband to make sure she took it, and went to bed.

He went into her bedroom and began the search himself. He found it buried deep in the pocket of a suitcase. I should have checked all the pockets of all the suitcases. That's where she hid it last time. Months ago, we were leaving the house for the airport when I saw her squirreling it away in the suitcase behind the closet. It took me a while to actually find it that time and we were so frantic to leave the house, we forgot to check on the cat and accidentally left him locked in a bedroom, having to wait until the following day to be rescued by our *ayah* who heard him meowing behind a closed door.

I was lying awake in the dark when my husband came to bed later. "I found it," he said. "I gave her a hug and told her I loved her." I felt the release and my hold on the anger subside. Thank you, Billy. Thank you for stepping up and finding the compassion. Thank you for your humor, too. I could not do this without you.

In the morning my mother would often awake with an unexplainable aggression. She stepped toward me and got inside my personal boundary, my space, she moved her body too close to mine, her face too close to my face. And when she was way too close for comfort, she'd give me the evil eye. And when I went to get her meds she'd accuse me of walking away from her, and then she would begin her list of complaints. She would not take a pain reliever or a hot shower or anything that I suggested to help her feel better.

She wants me to come into her room and feel the air. She's been fiddling with the remote for the AC, so yeah, it's kind of warm in there. I explain, once again, that if she's warm she has to push *this* button to get it cooler. Then I notice that the switch for the hot water heater on the wall outside of the bathroom is turned off. There's a little tab that says "heater" under the switch and there's a light that indicates it's on. It was off. "Mom, why is this off?" I ask her. "I turned that off in the middle of the night. Regina, my face. Look at how dry my skin is."

"Mom, that's for the *water* heater, so you'll have a hot shower."

"I always have a hot shower."

"That's because it's been on, but you have to *keep* it on."

"Regina, you don't understand. This is never on. If it were on then why do I always have hot water?"

"Mom, you just told me that you turned it off in the middle of the night!"

"Regina, I cannot swallow. I don't want that on!"

"Mom! This is for the *water* heater! It has nothing to do with the air in your room!"

"Then why is my face so dry?"

I want to tear out my hair. "I feel like I'm talking to a crazy person!" I yelled. I *am* talking to a crazy person. Walk away. Just walk away. I walked away. Then I came back.

"Mom, is there anything that I can say or do to convince you that water is separate from air?" I know that sarcasm is ridiculous, no matter how calm my voice is. I looked away from her. I paused a moment. I searched for the calm. I took some really deep breaths. "Mom, I made you a smoothie. Let's go have your smoothie." She followed me back into the kitchen where I poured her drink. Then I walked back into her bedroom and cut out a piece of paper and taped it over the word "heater" so it would no longer confuse her.

"Don't get sucked in to her drama." That was the advice a therapist I had seen in Peoria told me years ago. And here I was, not following his advice, getting sucked right in. But I *did* walk away. I walked away and then I changed the subject. I have to give myself some credit for that; and then remember to do that more often.

During those awful mornings when she woke up feeling miserable, she would ask me for the number to the hospital. She was used to numerous trips a week to the doctor's office when she lived in the US. We didn't need to do that any more. All she really wanted was a doctor to take her off her medicine. But unless there was an emergency, we were staying well away from the hospitals. What that meant, however, was that I was the only one she had to complain to, and to blame for her discomfort; I had to face her surly moods in the morning alone.

Billy says to her, "Miriam, you don't have any worries! It's time to enjoy life!" She's not entirely convinced that her retirement check is arriving in her bank account every month. "Like clockwork," Billy says to reassure her. "You should be sitting back and drinking a piña colada!"

She worries about money incessantly, which is weird because she will also give it away by the thousands. She'll send several thousand-dollar checks at a time to family members whom she knows are in need. She's always written checks for charity and she gives money to strangers on the street. When we lived in Rockville, Maryland, I was in the town square with her once when she started talking to a homeless man. She was kind of starting to look a little like a bag lady herself those days. Try as she did most of her life, she never shed her roots from poverty, and being older now and not caring as much, she has stopped making much of an effort. (Except in the lipstick department.)

She sat on a wall next to this man in the town square and struck up a conversation. I don't know what they were talking about but she laughed with him and I could tell she empathized. Then she handed him ten dollars and caught up with me. She's never forgotten how poor she once was nor has she forgotten the lack of food when she was a child. She won't leave food on a table at a restaurant. She hoards food in her purse; muffins, cookies, bread that's gone stale. She keeps a tight grip on the baggage she carries around with her from the Depression era.

And she's still convinced that she's left three checks behind in the retirement home. Every few days she will remind us of the drawer where she left them. We've lost count of all the credit cards she's cancelled because she was sure they were stolen when in fact she simply hid them somewhere. She called her bank and cancelled checks that she thought she lost, then she found them and used them until checks were bouncing all over the place. Finally, Billy took all banking issues out of her hands and deals with it himself, but every few days she still asks why she's not getting her bank statements. And the explanation of online banking starts up all over again. Billy patiently sits down with her again and shows my mom her bank account on the computer. It's a frustrating process for both of them and I tell him, "I don't know if it's worth it."

The one thing that we all want for Miriam is for her to be at peace—with life and with herself. We don't know if she will ever get there.

Chapter Twenty-One

Walking with my mom always gives me an opportunity to slow down and just be present with her. Sometimes we walk in silence; others times, we have great conversations.

Three men pass us on the street. I look at them and all three pairs of eyes are quietly fixed on my mom. I wonder what people are thinking when they see her. She is bent over and she does look old. People seem amazed that someone so old could be up and about! No one would guess at the lively conversations we often have, however. She is so present when I talk about the boys or about our plans for the future or even about memories from the past. She remembers a great deal; often she'll remember a name I've forgotten.

Like our Austrian neighbors who lived across the street from us for only a couple of years in Berea, but left their mark. I couldn't remember the father's name one day when I was thinking about them. "Albert," my mom informed me. "Albert Sturm." That was it! He was married to Alfreda and they had a son, Marcus.

Marry Me Stop

He was a drama teacher at Baldwin Wallace College. I was five and Marcus said he'd marry me when my hair got down to my knees. I think there was even a plastic engagement ring involved.

It was Alfreda who came over to sleep on our couch when my mother went into labor with my sister, Amiel. Alfreda delighted us several years in a row on Easter morning with enormous baskets filled with candy she left on our front porch for my brother and me. She gave my mother a ring once. That ring is on her finger today. And for me, she gave a handmade, woolen cape from Austria. I pulled it out of a box a few years ago for my son who had just watched "The Sound of Music" for the first time. He could have been one of the von Trapps in that cape.

Sadly, the Sturms left Berea when I was quite young, maybe six or seven, and moved to Vancouver, Canada. Many, many years later I was in Vancouver. I found a phone book and looked up the name Sturm. There was only one listed. I dialed, and Albert answered the phone. I was truly stunned at how easy it was to find him. "You're not going to believe who this is," I said to him after he said hello. "This is Regina, an old neighbor of yours. Do you remember me?" With hardly a pause he said, "How could I forget the little girl with red pigtails sitting on her tricycle?"

My then husband and I were invited to their home—still living elegantly—with a view of the harbor. Albert had left academia years ago and was now a cook on a tugboat. Alfreda managed a clothing boutique. Their son Marcus and his wife and their little girl were also at the gathering. What a fun reunion that was. It also prompted a visit from my mom, a few years later, to see her dear friends whom she never thought she'd see again.

My mom and I remember that reunion, and we talk about the coincidence of it all, of seeing them again after all those years. We talk about how easy it is to be in touch with people now, how great it is that we can Skype with Amiel and Barth and that we can email!

"What would we do without computers?" my mom says. "Pretty soon they'll put a man on the moon."

Pause.

"What do you mean, Mom? They've *put* a man on the moon."

"Well . . ." she realizes her mistake.

"About 45 years ago!"

"Oh."

We both laugh out loud. She has never lost her ability to laugh at herself.

I entered a writing contest. The question for the essay was, "What's the bravest thing you've ever done?" We talk about my answer to that question—leaving my first husband and joining the Peace Corps—and she listens compassionately. Round the park with my mom, I asked her what the bravest thing is that *she's* ever done. She starts talking about my father. How she was there for him when he died. But then she reconsiders. "The bravest thing I ever did was get on a boat for Holland when your father rejected me."

Even though she has told me that story countless times she added, "I can't remember how your father found the number to contact me." I remind her how and then tell her, "It's a good thing he found you cuz here we are." We look at each other and laugh. Yep. Here we are. In Dhaka, Bangladesh.

Marry Me Stop

"Who are you?" the little Bangladeshi boy says as he rides past me on his bike, circles back around me, and waits for an answer.

By now I know the common English mistakes, so I answer him,

"I'm fine thank you. How are you?"

"I'm fine tank you," he smiles in return, and watches us.

We continue walking and I turn around and say over my shoulder to him, "*Deka hobe!*" See you later!

My mom says to me, "You're so good with languages, Regina! I want to start learning some of the language."

"Well, Mom," I say, "do you remember the word you've already learned? Do you remember what *Na* means?"

"No."

I'm amazed she's remembered. "Right!" I exclaim. I pause, not quite sure. "So what does *Na* mean?"

"Right."

"No! It means *no*!"

"No?"

"Right!"

"As in left?"

It's a lost cause. And round and round we go.

Chapter Twenty-Two

Outside, a world of confusion and disorder still presses down on me. Sometimes men point a finger at me and I don't know why. Maybe it's because I am not wearing enough layers. I dress modestly, but I'm not dressed like the Bangladeshi women in *salwar kameez*, the loose pants and tunic and scarf to conceal the outline of the whole body. I ignore them and keep on walking. The cars and rickshaws and motorbikes, the men peeing against the walls, the beggars calling out to me at every turn in the road—Madaaaaaam!—makes me feel claustrophobic. I guess the one factor that lessens the pressure of this brutal assault of the environment comes in unlikely places: the faces of the people. A beggar points at his mouth, then at his grotesque, elephant-like leg, and then smiles at me. His very smile may be the one factor that earns him a living. Those smiles always soften my ventures outside.

I found other places to walk than just the park, paths around lakes, and different routes to different parks. I started looking around a bit more and noticing the foliage, the many flowers and tropical trees. I saw a monkey on a wall above me once. Then I saw one again on the path in front of me in the park. What a funny little thing, that monkey just walking along. A tall tree in the park is a home to giant bats. I can see them hanging from the branches with their wings tucked close and occasionally in the late afternoon they stretch from their long nap, their exotic, enormous wingspans unfolding above me.

It was all still a stinking mess, but it was becoming a more tolerable stinking mess. I was breathing more and learning to see things with different eyes. I stopped for a moment to peek at a domestic scene on a walk by a lake. A woman sitting on her haunches was stirring something over a clay oven built into the ground. It smelled spicy and good and I paused and watched her and smiled. She smiled at me, too, and then she offered me the pot. She held her pot of food out to me, insisting that I take some. I politely declined and kept walking. The poorest of the poor, offering me her food.

Going away gave us relief from the everyday assault of the heat, the pollution, and the poverty. In our first year, we left Dhaka four times for trips in the surrounding region. The highways are apparently so unsafe for driving in Bangladesh, the fatalities are so high, that the only way we risk leaving Dhaka is on a plane.

We went to Nepal for a long weekend. It's a one-hour flight from Dhaka. We went to Thailand during the winter break, a two-hour flight. We flew to Sri Lanka during the spring break, three hours away. We also went to the Sundarbans in southern Bangladesh.

All of these trips presented problems we did not anticipate before going, mostly around Miriam's conviction that someone was messing with her stuff. A necklace or a suitcase or a purse. Surprisingly, the one trip we seamlessly sailed through with my mother was the roughest one of all: the one on the boat with the man-eating crocodiles in the river below.

The Sundarbans have some of the largest mangrove forests in the world and the only real reason that most people go is in hopes of spotting a Bengal tiger. A few hundred are left, roaming around. The chances of seeing one are remarkably low, even though tour companies abound offering wildlife sightings. We went with several other families and I cannot imagine why one of the parents on this trip told her child that we're going on a boat so we can see a tiger. That is one set-up for disappointment.

I was the only person who got miserably ill on the three-day excursion. For the first 24 hours, I lay in the bowels of the boat, right next to the noxious-smelling gasoline tank, vomiting. The intermittent visits by my mom and Billy in my cabin were a relief. They were the only signs I had that life really exists off this wooden plank on which I was writhing.

By the second day, I climbed above deck. The fresh air helped, and I started to feel better. The boat was about to dock and we were going to go on a walk, through the forest and out to the Bay of Bengal. It would be quite a hike. Could I do it? Could my *mom* do it? Better than staying on the boat, I thought. Let's go.

We made it to the bay. I was doing fine by now. But the long hike back, with the sun high above us, was treacherous for my mom. Billy and a couple of the guides walked with her, someone on each side of her, holding her arm. They walked slowly, slowly. They stopped and rested in the shade of a tree. The rest of us were all at the boat by now, ready to go. Miriam and the guides and Billy were far, far behind. We waited and waited. The kids played in the dirt. No one was really in a hurry—there was nowhere to go except back on the boat anyway. People were patient. A Zen-like acceptance surrounded that waiting.

Someone said much later that Miriam was our lucky card that day. If we hadn't waited, if she hadn't taken her time and slowed us down, it never would have happened. The timing was impeccable. We all got back on the boat, sailed on down the river, and shortly afterwards our guide spotted it—an orange and white and black Bengal tiger, swimming across the river in front of our boat, roaring, showing its teeth, flexing its muscles and power, and then emerging from the water and up onto the banks of the river and vanishing into the thick of the trees. We were awed by the beauty. We hooted and hollered and jumped up and down. It was magical and we gave the credit for that unforgettable moment to the one who made us stop and slow down—Miriam.

Chapter Twenty-Three

O n the very last day of school, we flew back to Chicago. My mother was the only one in our household in our first year in Dhaka who did not get sick. I was sick almost every other month, mostly with various stomach problems and food poisoning, including dysentery. Mom breezed right on through.

So it was highly ironic that, after coming from a country where diarrhea is the number one killer, she'd get food poisoning the first week back in the States. From sushi. Ugh.

Her stomach—and mine—started feeling upset at almost the exact same time. The only difference is that I actually made it to the toilet. The night that followed was perhaps the single most difficult night I had caring for my mom—in the physically wretched sense.

From my bed in our condo where I lay groaning and moaning from my own discomfort, I could hear her coming down the hall. For the third or fourth time. Lord, please let her make it there, I prayed.

Marry Me Stop

She never did. How the hell she managed to crawl out of her bed and down the hall to the bathroom and then miss the toilet entirely I couldn't figure out. Shit was everywhere, on the floor, next to the toilet, *on* the toilet, just not *in* the toilet. I grabbed the paper towels, I grabbed the spray bottle, I was gagging from the smell, I was going to vomit from the smell.

Ohmygodohmygodohmygod. Fast! Get this over with as fast as possible. Spray. Wipe. Throw in plastic bag. "MOM! STOP!" She was starting to walk back to her bedroom with a nightgown covered in poop. I grabbed her. I was in military mode. I pulled the gown off her, trying not to get it in her hair. I ordered her to get in the shower. I turned the water on while she slowly tried to wash herself. Towel off. Find her more clothes. Get her back to bed. Throw dirty clothes in bucket. Run cold water over them. Dump water in toilet. Gag.

An hour later, repeat.

Somebody give me another *medal! Please!* Did my brother and sister *realize* what I was doing?

I lay in bed in the early morning, praying it was past. And I guess when it was finally all over, I thought about what this night would have been like for her if she had been alone. She may have been lying in her own excrement all night. In the end, it didn't really matter what I had just gone through. It was all over. Ultimately, I was relieved and glad that I was able to be there for her.

Like so many other times, too. I was relieved that my mom wasn't alone.

Back at the airport in Dhaka, Billy looked at me as we were waiting in line and said, "Round two." This was our second year back on a four-year assignment. We smiled at each other. We were resigned to our life here for now. Would we make the four rounds?

We wondered how many rounds my mom would make. Here she was again, with us on round two. So far, she was on a roll. Surprisingly, it wasn't as hard to return as I'd imagined it would be. Our cat was waiting for us. Our friend Olya left a casserole in our fridge. We exchanged summertime stories with friends. We *had* friends. Olya's husband, Jeff, and Billy were becoming best buds. My mom felt at home and was happy to be back in her bedroom. Hugging me goodnight she said, "Regina, I'm so lucky to have you."

She wondered where Gina was when we came back.

At the end of our first year in Dhaka, Gina and Louie moved back to the States. Gina was pregnant with their third child, and Louie's job here ended. Even though that was explained to my mother many times, whenever their names came up in conversation she still asked me when they are coming back. It was one of those things that just wouldn't sink in. Gina was such a burst of cheer and good humor that I think my mom mostly just didn't want to believe it. But Gina and I still talked on the phone or Skyped. I told my mom, "Gina called me this morning."

"Oh, that's nice. Now, when is she coming back to Dhaka?"

"She isn't."

"She's NOT coming back?"

"No, she's not coming back to Dhaka."

"To where?"

"To DHAKA. She's not coming back to Dhaka."

"Oh. That's too bad."

Miriam's short-term memory was shot. Sometimes we cannot help ourselves and it makes us all burst out laughing. When Ethan and my mom and I were sitting down at the American Club for lunch, she said to me, "Where is Gabriel?" I reminded her that he was at a sleepover. Seconds passed, then she turned to Ethan and said, "How was the sleepover?"

Ethan and I looked at each other and blurted out a laugh. "I'm not *Gabriel*," he said, chewing his hotdog. She laughed, too.

When Gabriel and Billy arrived and pulled chairs up to the table she said, "How was karate?" Gabriel told her, "I wasn't at karate. I was at a sleepover."

Boy, so confusing.

She may have lost her short-term memory, but she has not lost her sense of humor.

Her memory loss isn't always funny, however. My mother has a faraway look in her eyes sometimes, as if she knows she's going somewhere where there's no turning back. Her appearance is inward: stooped shoulders, sunken cheeks, even her eyes look like they are caving in. Sadness overcomes her at times when she ponders her loss. She still believes that all of her possessions are in a house in Ohio that's long been emptied of her dishes, her carpets, and her wall hangings. She forgets where she puts things, too, and at times this can lead to maddening conclusions, like her canceling her credit card when it was right there in her wallet, a blunder that took several weeks to resolve. When she's not defending her actions and when she's not arguing against reason, sometimes I see right to her sadness over her memory loss.

Regina Landor

She tells me she's lost her favorite necklace again. "And the necklace I was wearing today, that's gone, too," she says looking at me with a helpless expression. I glance around her room. "Mom! It's right there!" I say too loudly, pointing at her closet where it was hanging on a hook. "Oh," she says. She looks down at the floor and says quietly, "I just can't remember things." I look at her and I see her pain. Why I cannot always see it, I don't know. Why I cannot always respond softly to her confusion, her missteps, her forgetfulness, I don't know that either. I feel like my patience changes with every shift in the breeze and I regret every time I've gotten angry with her. Sometimes, she is my third child who follows me around the house asking me the same questions I have answered many times over.

We carefully packed her suitcase. Actually, we gave her my husband's smaller, more manageable bag for our second trip to Thailand. I helped her select several short-sleeved shirts, two pairs of pants, underwear, bra, and two necklaces. She could carry her eyeglasses, hearing aid case, and book in her purse. She wouldn't need a wallet. We had her passport. She needed very little for this six-day excursion. We were staying at a hotel in Bangkok for two nights, and a beach resort for three.

She waited by the front door, shoes on, purse in hand, pockets bulging. "Mom, let's just take two necklaces. Let's leave these at home." She complied as I took several necklaces out of her pockets. I opened her bag and checked it again. A stack of letters. I took those out, too. Less is more, or at least more manageable. I put the letters on her dresser in her room.

Marry Me Stop

On one of the trips we all took together, her missing neck-laces became the sole worry the entire time, and troubled us all. She claimed she packed them. As I was the one who helped her pack, I knew that she hadn't. She blamed the hotel staff for taking them. She blamed the airlines. She was frantic. On our last day, we actually found them: she had hidden them in her eyeglass case, and she never wears her glasses.

We arrived at our new destination. Our beach cottage was clean and airy. She said she liked the room. She told me I'm so good at planning the right place to stay. The most surprising thing about what she said next was the utter lack of any trace of humor in her voice. It surprises me that even now I can be so taken aback by her delusions. "That's not my suitcase," she said, staring down at her suitcase. Because it was her suitcase, at least the one that we packed together in her room less than 24 hours ago, that sentence should have been funny.

I wanted to hear the resignation creep into her voice. Or a laugh when I pointed out that these are her clothes. I started rifling through the bag. Here were her letters! She snuck them in after all. This time I was glad to see them, physical proof that this is her bag. "Look, Mom. Your letters. This is from Aunt Ann. This is your bag." She shook her head, unconvinced. The resignation never came.

Instead, on each day of our holiday, she woke up with a fur-rowed brow, complaining despairingly about her lost bag. "We need to go to the front office," she said as we walked barefoot in the sand along the edge of the Gulf of Thailand.

"What for, Mom?" I asked her.

"To see about my bag. Maybe someone has turned it in." I pointed out the figure of Gabriel in the distance, standing up on a wooden swing, swinging in the branches like an acrobatic monkey. It was a joy to see my boys soak up this outdoor playground, playing in the sand and the water all day long. Their bodies naturally yearned for space, coming from the cramped environs of Dhaka. My mom looked up; maybe she smiled slightly, just barely acknowledging her grandson. She just barely acknowledged any of her surroundings on that trip.

The cloud of despair descended so completely on my mother that week I thought for sure that this was it. I thought her depression had spiraled to a place of no return. She never got over thinking that someone had taken her bag.

And then we came back to Dhaka. We walked out of the airport and there was Mahabub, our trusty driver, ready and waiting with our big, white van.

We piled in and took off, back towards the traffic circle and the barefoot children, the mothers with half-drugged babies on their shoulders, the man with a grotesquely hunched back and a cane, the maimed and the deformed. I was in that familiar place again, that crossroads of what we had just left behind, the luxury of our resort and the dregs of humanity. I braced myself as we got closer to the traffic circle. My stomach felt tight.

Then I looked over at my mom expecting to see that familiar frown of unease. But that's not what I saw, and I was amazed. The cloud had disappeared. She was actually smiling at me. Smiling! She was wearing her fuchsia-colored long-sleeved tee shirt she bought with me last summer at Ann Taylor. Cheerful once again, clearly happy to be back, happy to be going toward our apartment and familiar surroundings, in that moment she looked more beautiful than ever.

Chapter Twenty-Four

In some ways, my mother has become a child again. She's reverted to the time when she was a little girl in New Jersey, about to be punished for something she didn't know she did. But now there is no one around to punish her, so it seems that the only other option she has is to punish herself.

She tells herself she needs to lead the two-hour discussion during her Bible study group, when no such thing is true. Nothing I say will convince her otherwise, nothing I say, nothing the women in the group say. So each week, before she goes off to her study group, she will fret because she has not prepared properly. Her anxiety is extreme. She paces. She wrings her hands. She approaches me filled with worry, fear, and sadness over not having prepared. She combs through her Bible and takes notes up until the moment she is to walk out the door. She's a child again about to go off to school, unprepared.

Character traits that were always present in my mother have become exacerbated in her declining state. Like her love of clothes. She likes to shop, she likes getting new clothes, and she loves getting a bargain. But at times they become an obsession. Not in getting new ones, but in the clothes that she already has. She thinks most of her clothes were stolen. Many of them were given away, at her request. When we were clearing out her things before moving, I held up each item to see which ones she'd like to keep and which ones she'd like to give to Goodwill. But she doesn't remember that. She only remembers that a top/blouse/ sweater/pair of pants that she used to have in her closet is not there anymore.

She believes the clothes that are in her closet no longer fit her. They do fit her. She puts on a pair of pants, looks down at her feet and says to me, "Look at these, Regina." I look.

"Mom, those fit you. Any shorter, you'd be wearing high-waters. You'd look like a nerd. Do you want to look like a nerd?" God, what's wrong with me? Sometimes sarcasm is the only way I can hold on to my sanity.

Tailors are on just about every street corner and marketplace in Dhaka. Tailors abound like tropical trees here. Everyone enjoys the fruits of their labor, and not just westerners. Bangladeshis go to the tailors like Americans go to Target.

So I give in. I take my mom to the tailor's with all the skirts and pants that she thinks are too long. We'll get them hemmed, even though I sense this isn't the end of it, because in truth, they don't need to be hemmed. But it's easy and I want her to be happy.

Oh, how my intuition is so often correct. Of *course* that wasn't the end of it. A month later, those same clothes that we brought to the tailor, that the tailor actually hemmed for her to the length she specified, those same damn clothes were back in a pile on the floor to be brought to the tailor to be hemmed!

Ahhhhhh!!! Save me from the madness!

I won't bother repeating the circular discussions I had with her and my futile attempts to get her to *see* the madness, but I ask you to imagine them. (Just imagine the words, not the part where I was close to tears.)

Sometimes I need some relief from it.

I want to go on a walk. I desperately need some exercise and a friend has just called. I'm meeting her in a few minutes. My mom just got up from bed and I don't want her to see me. She will slow me down. She's gone on the balcony to drink her coffee. I go into my bedroom and when I come out she's standing in the living room and she sees me. I tell her I'm going on a walk. "I want to come with you," she says.

"Not this time. I'm going to walk fast."

"I'll walk fast." No, she wouldn't. Either Mahabub or I will take her on a walk later, and I'm going to take her with us to our friend's for dinner tonight. I am determined not to feel guilty about this. Plus, it's noon and she hasn't eaten a thing yet. I put on my shoes.

"Look at my face, Regina. Look at the wrinkles on my face! Regina, I think I'm having a reaction to the medicine!" She grips her face with her hands.

"Mom, you're almost *eighty*. You're supposed to have wrinkles. Go eat breakfast," I say as I walk out the door.

Marry Me Stop

All along, it's been important to me to let her read as much of this story as I feel she can handle. I want her to be as much a part of this process as she is able. Her short-term memory may be gone, but a lot of her long-term memory is still intact. "I retired in 1996," she told me the other day. Her long-term memory has helped me in much of the telling of this story.

But it's not all her story. It's also mine. And I don't know how much I'm willing to have her read, if drawing attention to her declining state is worth the pain it could invoke. So I'm tentative about what I show her. Sometimes, she will talk about her father and be adamant that he meant well. She insists that I need to say that he started a love and peace movement, with a capital L and a capital P. She doesn't want me to say one word about a razor belt. I didn't want to argue with her about that. I asked her, "Do you just want me to write that your father was a good, loving man and stop there?" She pauses, so conflicted about her past. We talk about how our parents wound us, however unintentional that is. That her father left wounds. That my father left wounds. It's what happens. Maybe each generation that passes gets a little better at parenting, but I still recoil at the thought of the wounds I will be leaving my own children.

My mother doesn't want to betray her father. She tells me that his anger is not what defined him—that he wanted love. That he believed in world peace. She begs me to understand this, and what I understand above all else is that, like my own father, her father was a complicated man. But he also hurt her and her siblings, and it's this that she is unwilling to look at, face on. Decades and decades later, she is holding on to her conviction that he was a good man.

The abuse that he inflicted has its ramifications. Whether or not she is willing to acknowledge this, the wounds have stayed with her. She frets and she broods and she is not at peace. She will not forgive that little girl that lives inside of her—that little girl that yearns to be acknowledged and loved—for doing whatever it is that she did wrong, or thought she did wrong. It's time to accept yourself, I tell her. They are the same words she would have told me years earlier.

My everlasting hope is that one day my mom will feel as good about herself as she made others feel about themselves. She is self-deprecating—sometimes to a fault. Even though she was a fabulous cook when I was growing up, I never heard her brag about a thing. When she went to a high school reunion—maybe her fiftieth—an old classmate told her that he thought she was the smartest person in school. "I was so shocked when he told me that. I never thought of myself as smart," she tells me.

She has always helped others feel good about themselves and she's always been my biggest fan. She thinks I'm wonderful—at being a mother, at cooking, at organizing my life, at everything. She marvels out loud at my ability to make friends, to write, to raise my kids, and to keep in touch with people. When we are in a group setting and we're going around the circle introducing ourselves, the first thing my mother usually says is, "Regina is my daughter." Being a mother defines her. "I'm so lucky to have you," she tells me again and again.

My mother has moments of utter clarity and lucidity. She can still listen to me if I have a problem. She listens to the boys. One of her favorite times of the day is when Ethan and Gabriel have their violin practice. She is in awe of her grandsons. She marvels at how they've improved in their playing. She nods her head as she listens; she smiles at me as their bows glide over the strings.

Some things may never be resolved inside my mother. She may always fret and feel anxious. Even though I believe that it is never too late to accept life the way it is, it may never happen for her. It's possible she may not achieve the peace that we long for her to feel.

But it's also possible that she'll have a shot at getting there if we stop trying to resist who she is becoming and how she is declining. I think the only chance for my mother to move closer to that place of peace is if we walk there with her. I am learning to agree with almost everything she says. If she tells me that her necklace is missing, my inclination now is to hold her hand, look her in the eyes and say, "I'm sorry. That's really sad. That was your favorite necklace." She is profoundly grateful to be heard, and then I change the subject. I'll find something to distract her, like a flower if we're outside on a walk, and I'll ask her to smell its fragrance.

The journey we're on is not easy. There's a lot of hand-holding involved. We always seem to be taking a few steps forward and then a step back. That's because there are many potholes to avoid. There's traffic in the way, blocking our vision. There's mud and there's grime and there's dust and there's rubble and sometimes it just plain stinks. But then there's a smiling face in the distance, there's a kind gesture and someone makes a terrific joke, and there's a glimpse at a magnificent animal in the water. And we then feel ever closer to our goal. The journey is hard and the journey is long. But, oh man, the journey is so worth it in the end.

Epilogue

Not long ago, we were invited to the home of a Bangladeshi family for dinner. The woman is the director of one of the schools that we bring food to in the slums. She and her family live in an apartment nearby. In the Muslim tradition, we all sat and ate while she stood the whole time, serving us. Her husband talked about his own family and his parents. And we talked about my mother, while she sat at the table eating and listening. He told me, like many, many other Bangladeshi people have told me, that I am so very lucky to have my mother. And then he said something that I thought was profound and that I had not yet heard. He told me that in the Koran it is considered a great deed—the greatest deed—to care for a parent. That if that task falls upon you, you are the fortunate one.

In many ways, I feel like I am the fortunate one. Not always, but often. On my journey of going there, of walking with her to that place of peace, I'm hoping to arrive at that place of peace myself. Maybe we're both helping each other get there. I look at her sitting in our living room, and she is here, even though it seems she is often fading in and out. She is present now, and I want to cherish her presence, because I know she won't always be here. And maybe we won't always be the ones caring for her. But we are now and I feel lucky for us, for my boys, and grateful for Billy's compassion and good humor.

In March, Billy and I hosted a surprise party for my mother's eightieth birthday. Friends came to honor her and give her gifts. Billy led her upstairs, she turned the corner, and we all shouted,

"Surprise!" Even though hours earlier we were all cooking and preparing and frantically getting ready for a surprise party around her, she was *completely* surprised. Our friend, Meredith, made two cakes depicting aspects of her life with chocolate fondant: a suitcase, an airplane, and the Jersey Shore. Another friend, Sabine, found someone in Dhaka to design a hand-shaped cookie cutter. Representing the hands of the children that my mother has helped wash in the slums, and the number of years of her life, she presented her with a tray of eighty hand cookies. My mother felt honored and loved and was delighted by it all.

Before starting this trip overseas, her doctor in Evanston said that he wouldn't recommend it. It would be better if he could continue monitoring her medicine and her brain on a monthly basis. But he also understood that her quality of life was a factor, too. She had to weigh the two factors: the importance of monthly brain monitors in a state-of-the-art hospital or going on a wild adventure with her family whom she loves. For my mom, that decision was, thankfully, a simple one. Bangladesh? *Let's goooooo!*

33842695R00124

Made in the USA
Columbia, SC
11 November 2018